work rooms

Fay Sweet

work rooms

PLANNING YOUR SPACE AND WORKING IN STYLE

First published in 2000 as *Home.Work* by Conran Octopus Ltd
a part of Octopus Publishing Group
2–4 Heron Quays, London E14 4JP
www.conran-octopus.co.uk

This paperback edition published in 2004

Commissioning editor Catriona Woodburn
Managing editor Helen Ridge
Senior art editor Carl Hodson
Picture research Liz Boyd
Special photography Winfried Heinze
Styling for special photography Abigail Ahern
Illustrator Paul Williams
Production Alex Wiltshire

A catalogue record is available for this book
from the British Library

ISBN 1 84091 395 9

Printed in China

contents

introduction

When I moved into my current house ten years ago, I was the only person in the street who worked at home. Today my homeworking neighbours include another journalist, a book editor, an architect, a translator, a violin-maker, a solicitor, a textile designer and a stained-glass artist. The upside of this change is that the street is a more sociable place to live; on the downside there are now queues in the delicatessen at lunchtime.

There is no question that the pattern of work is changing. Companies are unable to offer jobs for life, and growing numbers of people are employed on short-term contracts or have chosen the independence of being self-employed. At the same time, the opportunities to work from home have been enhanced by new technology: cheaper and more efficient computers and advances in telecommunications make it much easier to work away from the corporate hub and in your own remote home office.

Working from home has a powerful allure. It offers flexibility and control. Most of my neighbours had been employed in corporate offices before they decided to work at home. The solicitor, for example, decided to set up on her own after she was made redundant, while the violin-maker opted out of a steady job as a civil engineer to follow his passion for making musical instruments.

The increase in homeworking is sure to continue. In 1994 around 40 million Americans were estimated to be working at home; by the turn of the century the figure was closer to 60 million, with around half using the home to catch up on work from the office and one-third running their own businesses. In the UK, it is predicted that by 2006 more than 30 per cent of the workforce will be working at home.

going to work

Take control of your work and

your office space and improve

your quality of life

who are homeworkers?

With doors to the garden and walls hung with favourite paintings, this office gives a glimpse of how enjoyable working at home can be. In addition to being a welcoming and pleasing environment, it is also well equipped, with ergonomically designed chairs, generous worktop space and good-quality lighting.

Homeworkers are drawn from dozens of spheres: along with the homemakers and child carers there is an ever-expanding spectrum of other professions. Most homeworkers are self-employed; many, such as designers and writers, are from the creative world, but there are others with jobs as varied as acupuncturists, sewing machinists and computer software writers. Then there are those who use their home as a base but carry out their work elsewhere,

for example, decorators, electricians, gardeners, plumbers and musicians. The remaining group, and one that is growing rapidly, is that of the teleworker, or company employee, who works full- or part-time at home but who receives a company salary.

This book cannot possibly hope to embrace all types of work carried out in the home but, given that most homeworkers use a computer some or all of the time, it is aimed at those who are desk-based.

I have worked at home for more than 15 years and, like many people, started out on the kitchen table. I kept my computer on a trolley, so that it could be wheeled away out of sight at the end of the day. I then moved into a corner of my bedroom. To contain the office, I designed a tall desk unit, complete with shelves and filing drawers, which could be closed up when it was not in use. As my collection of books and files continued to expand, I took over the box room, but eventually moved house and had an entire bedroom for my office. Interestingly, with the latest technology offering mobile phones, hand-held computers with built-in modems and portable printers, my office needs are shrinking. I still own many reference books and magazines, which have to be stored somewhere, but I can (and do) work just about anywhere.

Taking the decision to work at home can be one of the best moves you will make in life. It opens up the opportunity to take control of your time, your workload and your work environment. You will have the flexibility to work when you want for as long as you want. You will have a greater choice of what you do and how you do it. But working from home is not a soft option if you want to earn a living. To be successful requires discipline, self-motivation and self-sufficiency in working alone for days at a time. It is also important to realize that by importing an office into the home, you will probably have to cope with a change in lifestyle as the boundaries between work and home-life become less clearly defined. Most of the change will be for the better, but beware of the pitfalls of allowing work to take over your life and your living space.

One of the benefits of working at home is that you can create the office you have always wanted, to reflect your personality and your working needs exactly.

changes in the workplace

While working at home is certainly a recent and growing phenomenon, it is far from being a new idea. Before the birth of corporate life and the offices and factories spawned by the industrial revolution, it was the norm to work from home. Artisans carried out their work in home-based workshops, families farmed together, milled flour, brewed beer, wove cloth, even ran shops on the premises where they lived. Working from home applied to the professionals, too, including doctors, lawyers, the clergy and bankers.

In the late 19th and early 20th centuries, the new workplaces in offices and factories drew people away from home and obliged them to commute to their places of employment. For the employee, the dull workhalls were an anonymous backdrop to the modern imperative of mass production. We are all quite familiar with the grainy black-and-white photographs of serried ranks of clerical workers (at first, mostly male) in stiff, workday clothes, bent over their ledgers. These human hothouses of activity were run on ferociously strict lines, and the jobs were often mind-numbingly repetitive, but at least they guaranteed a regular wage.

Matters improved after the Second World War, when office employers began to realize that a more sympathetic environment actually encouraged a more productive workforce. Stylish office furniture started to be designed and offices were made brighter and more comfortable.

During the 1960s and 1970s, rents for town-centre locations rocketed and many companies relocated to semi-rural and suburban locations, to new, purpose-built business parks. Interiors took on

It is difficult to imagine anyone looking forward to a day's work in this office. It is oppressive and probably noisy, the rows of desks are packed very closely together, the lighting is dismal and the work undoubtedly monotonous. An office like this would be totally unacceptable today as we recognize the importance of the working environment and know that happy people are productive people.

The boundaries are blurring between home and office. In this corporate office the reception area boasts playground swings and a grass lawn. Research has shown that we work best in relaxed environments, and it is not unusual to see sofas, rugs, lamps, piles of magazines and even games, such as table football.

a softer look, old-fashioned rigid hierarchies were challenged, and open-plan spaces provided a less formal working environment.

By the 1980s and 1990s office design had been elevated virtually to the status of a science. Interior architects and designers started to talk about office landscaping, internal 'streets', creative spaces, hubs for exchange, ergonomic workstations, hotdesking, soft areas for brainstorming, 'monks' cells' for quiet thought, colour schemes to stimulate or subdue, even 'break-out' areas for play and to relieve stress. Gradually the corporate office has become less formal and hierarchical, and changed in style and comfort to look more and more like the home .

Running alongside changes in office style have come the rapid and overwhelming advances of the technological revolution. The old ways of thinking have been altered irrevocably. In the new age, the once-expensive and space-consuming technology has shrunk to become compact and inexpensive. Anyone can own a home computer and access the

rest of the globe via the internet. It is no longer necessary for companies to import a workforce daily to an office building in order for it to work as a unit. An information-based society knows no boundaries. The virtual office has arrived.

Flexi-time, part-time working and job-sharing are now appealing options for many office workers. Although there are companies that still find it hard to accept that their staff will work hard when at home and unsupervised, plenty of others have made the leap of faith. The corporate culture is switching away from the need to see employees sitting at their desks, and towards being more interested in seeing the results of their work.

Many employees of enlightened companies work at home some of the time while remaining linked to their offices by telephone and computer. And plenty work at home full-time as teleworkers, carrying out phone- and computer-based work, running advice and technical support lines for manufacturers, sending out brochures and taking orders for mail-order and internet-based companies, selling insurance policies and processing claims, operating nationwide telephone services for car breakdown organizations, and even running banks.

For those workers who have gone one step further and chosen self-employment, there is a trade-off for the greater sense of freedom that being your own boss offers: the self-employed have to be self-sufficient. There is no sick pay or holiday pay, and the law requires you to present your yearly accounts to the tax office, as well as meeting all the costs of setting up in business and being responsible for your own training, sales and marketing.

is homeworking right for you?

Working from home offers an enormous range of benefits. The greatest advantage of being self-employed is that you are in control of your working life, so you can run it as you like. But before setting out you should ask yourself a number of questions: first, do you have space to accommodate a home office, and do you have a budget for decorating, furnishing and equipping that space?

Then there is the matter of the business plan. In setting up any business you should be confident that your chosen enterprise will work and provide the required income. A business plan is a means of assessing whether your proposal is viable. It is a speculative exercise, but provides a framework to compare all possible expenditure with all possible income, and to test whether the business will work. The plan should also include a realistic forecast of income and expenditure for the coming three years, to suggest ways in which the business might flourish, even expand, to guarantee a livelihood. As well as working out your proposals on paper it is always a good idea to test plans by discussing them with friends and an accountant.

To progress the idea, be sure there is a buyer for your services or goods. Have you identified potential customers and discussed your plans with

word association

In a Work at Home seminar conducted at London's Royal College of Art, participants were invited to collect together words and phrases that they closely associated with home and work. Taking part were students, designers, journalists and professionals involved in the business of teleworking. The object of the exercise was to explore how we view these two areas of life, and to promote debate about how home and work might be accommodated under the same roof. Following the seminar, a research group has been formed on the product design course at the college; its brief is to pursue research and development related to this important social change.

TEN MOST POWERFUL IMAGES OF HOME	TEN MOST POWERFUL IMAGES OF WORK
Comfortable	Pressure
My room/belongings	Stress/busy/fast pace
Love/family	Creative
Peace/quiet/private	Social environment/people
Relaxed	Telephone
Safe	Technological systems
Warmth	Efficiency/decisions/juggling
Enjoyment/stress-free	Team/consultation/meetings
Food	Information overload
Bed/sleep	Office politics

them? Only by carrying out this rudimentary but essential market research can you be reassured that the business will provide financial security, even during what may be an unstable start.

And question your own skills and approach: do you need more training, are you self-motivated and disciplined enough to get up and get going every day? Most people new to the self-employed and freelance life find coping with loneliness the most difficult aspect of their new work. Do you think that you will be able to work alone for long periods of time without becoming demotivated?

Inevitably there will be some really gloomy times. Are you prepared for the difficult moments of setting up a new business when things do not go as planned? Most people need an adjustment period of between 30 and 90 days before they feel really comfortable with the changes they have made and their new working life. It is therefore important to build in strategies to cope with the two key troublesome areas in the early days: loneliness and slow cashflow. It will almost certainly be tough at the outset, but if you are prepared and determined, working at home can become a real opportunity to enhance your quality of life.

LEFT *Because isolation and loneliness are often identified as the greatest problems facing new homeworkers, sharing your office space can provide welcome company. With growing numbers of us working at home, whether full time or part time, it is not unusual for partners to share a home office, such as the one featured here.*

OPPOSITE *Working at home need not be lonely. Many self-employed people team up with colleagues for specific projects and hire in part-time staff to help at busy times.*

eyes wide open

On the face of it, working from home offers huge benefits in the quality of life. These are just some of the reasons why people choose to set up a home office. However, for every plus there is usually a minus. It is worth remembering that there may be difficult times ahead. Taking the decision to work from home is not a soft option, so look before you leap.

ADVANTAGES OF WORKING AT HOME	DISADVANTAGES OF WORKING AT HOME
Independence from the office system (and office politics)	Isolation from fellow workers
Fewer office distractions	Loss of opportunity for regular social exchanges with colleagues
Greater productivity	Possible loss of status outside the office environment
Control over your working life	Lack of access to a full range of office equipment
The option of saying 'no' to work you do not want to take on	Difficulty of effectively managing your own time
Control over your work environment	Too many distractions, such as interruptions from partner, children and neighbours
Flexibility to work when you want	Feeling of being constantly surrounded by work
No commuting	Temptation to work evenings, weekends and any spare time you may have
Reduced stress levels	
More time with the family	Bearing the cost of equipment, furniture, stationery, extra heating and lighting
Possible tax advantages	

what to avoid

The disadvantages of setting up a home office certainly look daunting, so it is useful to know how to minimize the negatives. Isolation is a major concern for those just starting out on their own, but there are many ways to alleviate it. You can establish small networks with others working in the same field or neighbourhood, or make contact through professional associations, advertisements in work-related publications or by putting a notice in a newsagent's window. Make sure you build in regular trips to suppliers, such as the post office, newsagent and stationer, and make an effort to get to know your local shopkeepers and neighbours. It can also be worthwhile attending work-related open days, exhibitions, trade shows or functions where you are likely to make new contacts.

Another major problem suffered by home-based workers is marking and keeping clear office boundaries. One of the first steps to take is installing a dedicated office phone line with an answering machine that has a volume control dial; turn it right down out of work hours and you will probably not even hear it ring. For those lucky enough to have a whole room to devote to an office, there is no excuse for work-related material spilling over into the living area. However, if your office is part of another room, a great deal of discipline is required to stop papers and office matter spreading. But there are ways to prevent this. Keep archive material packed away and stored elsewhere in the home. Try not to let paperwork mount up; the regular clearing of files and in-trays should impose some control. And, if possible, spend ten minutes at the end of each day clearing your desk of all extraneous items.

Not only will this reduce the temptation to work into the evening, but it will also make the desk more welcoming the next morning.

Then there is the matter of how many hours you should work. Of course, working at home gives you the freedom to work the hours you prefer, but studies show consistently that homeworkers tend to spend more time at their desks than their office-based colleagues. It is important to create an outline work timetable and stick to it. Let others know your plan, and try to resist distractions such as childcare and visiting friends within your designated work timeframe. Where possible avoid working during the evenings when your company will be expected by partners, family and friends. Unless you are determined to be a hermit, it is incredibly unhealthy to neglect your social life.

Among the commonest problems encountered by new businesses is badly judged investment at the outset. The start-up budget should always include enough to buy the right basic equipment and allow for the possibility of a slow cashflow during the first few months, at least while the business is being established. Too often the temptation is to spend lavishly on equipment and not allow enough time for the first months of slow trading. The golden rule remains that the bank balance should be checked thoroughly before any major expenditure.

With the home office becoming more and more a fact of home life, don't feel compelled to hide it away. This office has been made as a beautiful, freestanding box within the living space. It is almost like an enormous framed picture, and is clearly marked off from the living space by its walls and the single step up to the work platform.

practicalities

The best way to establish a

business at home is by investing

time in thorough planning

assessing your needs

A simple workspace in a shared room is ideal for those who work only part time at home. In this living room, a small and discreet office has been built from the same materials as the adjacent shelving. However, even the simplest office needs adequate storage and a generous worktop.

Unlike most office workers, people who work at home have the opportunity and luxury of creating their own tailor-made, ideal work environment. If you like working in a huge creative muddle, then that's just fine; equally, if you want to reduce your work environment to an empty white cube, then why not? Whatever your choice, it is important to establish a plan for the kind of office you need, can afford and have room for.

The basic requirements that an office must meet are a comfortable space with a good-quality chair, a generous work surface, the appropriate equipment, adequate storage space and, if possible, plenty of natural light. The workstation, no matter how small, should be well designed and attractive, to encourage you to work.

Start off by listing the equipment you know you will need for everyday work. For most desk-based jobs this will usually mean a computer, printer and telephone. Depending on the work you do, additional items to consider might include a fax machine or a laptop docking station. For most jobs, there will be equipment that is useful but less frequently required. Items needed less than once a week, such as a photocopier, might be best left off the list, especially when there is limited space and a modest budget. In any case, a trip to the local library or stationers to use their photocopier can be a useful and enjoyable break from desk work.

After these basics, extra items will depend on the type of work being undertaken. And storage requirements will vary. Writers and editors are likely to need generous shelving space for reference books and magazines, and a filing system for archive material, while accountants, secretaries and solicitors will need deep shelves for files and plenty of remote storage for past projects. Designers and illustrators, on the other hand, may need plan chests for large sheets of paper and extra large desktop space for sketching and drawing. Work out whether you have any unusual requirements such as lockable cabinets for expensive or sensitive equipment, and air-tight or fireproof cases for precious documents and data.

When evaluating storage, always overestimate; if you have ever had to move work premises, you will remember the unbelievable number of crates it takes to empty even a modest office.

Begin to assess how much space this will all require. If your office needs are fairly minimal, then perhaps a workstation of desk and chair can be accommodated in a spare bedroom/hallway/corner of the living room. This is more likely to be a good solution if you work only part time. Of course, if you have plenty of spare space, dual-purpose rooms are not an issue, and for the full-time worker, whose needs are likely to be greater with so much work paraphernalia, a separate office is essential; it could be depressing and counterproductive to try to work in a cramped area. Where space is really limited you

It may appear a great luxury to have an entire room dedicated solely as a home office, but if you work at home full time, it does help focus attention to have a space that is separate from the rest of the house. It also means that at the end of the day it will be easier to close the door behind you and forget about work.

OPPOSITE *Now you see it, now you don't. This brilliantly clever minimal office is hinged to the wall and stands on wheels, so that it can be opened out when needed and closed up when not. It is a neat space ideal for short bursts of work.*

RIGHT *Full-time jobs almost always require large amounts of reference material and storage space. This opened-up room has an entire wall given over to shelving and includes a generous worktop, which doubles as a meeting table. Converted space at the top of a building brings in excellent natural light to illuminate a room.*

may be better off hiring an office outside the home. Alternatively, perhaps there is the opportunity to invest in converting the attic, building a small extension or converting a garden shed?

There are other considerations, too. Will you be working alone or do you expect to hire in additional help on a part-time or occasional basis? Is there enough room to accommodate another person? Do you expect regular visits from clients? Is a meeting room or a presentation area a requirement? Perhaps a separate entrance for business guests would be a good idea? If you need to spend a lot of time on non-computer-based activities such as reading reports, a soft seating area could be a welcome addition in your office. And think about the irritants that might break your concentration. Do you need absolute silence and solitude for long periods of time, or can you work with occasional disruptions?

Think about how the space will be presented. Would you like your office to be well ordered and sober, or should it look contemporary and creative? The choice of décor will certainly send out powerful messages about you and the type of work you do:

an uncared-for environment, for example, will not only be uninspiring to work in day after day, but it will also suggest to visiting clients that you take correspondingly little care in the work you do. Ask yourself, too, whether you want the office area to be in keeping with the rest of the house, or to have a separate personality of its own. Take account of what you like about other people's offices, and what you dislike. And if you already have an office, work out exactly what annoys you about it. Can it be put right, or is it back to the drawing board?

The quality of your workspace will always be affected by light. Natural light makes a comfortable environment, but it will need to be supplemented by an artificial lighting scheme. Since the most effective light levels for desk-based work are stronger than those elsewhere in the home, lighting needs careful consideration; poor lighting can cause eyestrain, flatten moods and consequently reduce productivity. You will not only need to add overall room illumination, but also task lamps or desk lamps, to highlight areas of close-up activity.

tools of the trade

This check box is intended as a starting point for determining which equipment you should have at the outset and which you could safely buy at a later date. Some of the tools listed below may be completely inappropriate for your line of work, and a vital piece of equipment may have been omitted: for example, a fabric designer will obviously need a different range of work tools from a journalist. But whatever your profession, when setting up in business beware of spending lavishly on too many tempting but unnecessary gadgets, and be clear about the minimum amount of equipment you need to start with, to complete your work effectively.

EQUIPMENT NEEDED FOR EVERYDAY WORK
Computer with keyboard and mouse
CD-ROM drive
External modem
Laptop docking station
Printer
Telephone/answering machine
Intercom
Mobile phone and charger
Fax machine
Filing cabinet and files
Desklamp
In-tray
Pen holder

Desk diary/calendar
Noticeboard
Radio/hi-fi system

EQUIPMENT NEEDED OCCASIONALLY
Image scanner
Desktop bookrest or document holder
Portable television and video recorder
Digital camera
Desk-mounted pencil sharpener
Tape dispenser
Spiral binder
Photocopier
Desk fan

OPPOSITE *We all respond positively to sunlight. This industrial building was designed and built with high ceilings and enormous metal-framed windows to allow the maximum amount of natural light to fall on the workers inside. Now that the building has been converted into living units, this space has become the perfect home office.*

assessing your needs

This is also a good moment to consider how your home may need to change to accommodate an office. Is your electrical wiring in good condition and able to cope with new and increased demands from additional electrical equipment? Do you need to invest in a burglar alarm and improved security with better locks?

Always remember that in setting up your own home office you are liberated from the tyranny of someone else's poor design and lack of thought. If you get it wrong, you have only yourself to blame.

the good, the bad and the ugly

As you start to build a list of your needs, it becomes possible to create an idea of context, and you will begin to see how everything might fit together. For more inspiration where better to look than the best and worst of corporate offices? In any design challenge it helps to identify bad points as well as the good, so you know what to avoid. Think of the big issues, like storage, and comfort, as well as smaller considerations, such as how to organize your filing, where to position your desk lamp, and even where to put your coffee cup.

PLUS POINTS OF CORPORATE OFFICES	NEGATIVE POINTS OF CORPORATE OFFICES
Large desks with plenty of worksurface	Poor ventilation and fixed windows
Comfortable chairs	Lack of natural light
Big windows	Uninspiring and bland colour schemes
An outside view, visible while sitting down	Ugly furniture
A variety of storage units that can cope with everything from large files to a stapler	Shallow desktops
	Chest-level movable partitions
Coffee machine and water dispenser close by	Noise disturbance
Fax machine and printer close to the desk	Desk lamps that cannot be angled
Hands-free telephone headset	Inadequate storage for small items
Space for plants and flowers	Shelves too shallow to accommodate large books and box files
Pictures on the wall	
Deep filing cabinets	Badly managed filing systems
Good quality files with tough plastic labels	Piles of unused paper and reports
Appropriate levels of ambient and task lighting	Desks without drawers
Floor sockets for electrical equipment	Messy wiring

ABOVE *If all you need is a minimal office with a desk, chair and computer, then keep things simple. In a shared-use room, a folding screen is an effective and attractive way of separating the office from the living space.*

OPPOSITE *In an industrial-style interior there is no need to be constrained by convention as the traditional room plan does not exist. Make the most of the flexibility and create spaces to suit the way you live and work. Here, an office has been cleverly built into a dividing wall.*

identifying your office space

With a picture emerging of what your home office might contain comes the necessity to find a space to accommodate it. The temptation can often be to relegate an office to a far-flung corner of the home – after all, rarely is a home office housed in a room of great size and beauty, and we may feel that if the computer is out of sight, it will also be out of mind. But there is a dilemma: if your office is where you intend spending your working life and earning your living, shouldn't it be a high-quality environment that you enjoy being in? Of course, a balance must be maintained: the work area shouldn't dominate the living space, but neither should it be shoved into a dark and unappealing corner.

The classic home office location is in the guest bedroom. If you have the luxury of this extra space, it makes excellent use of a room that is otherwise almost certainly under-used; many guest rooms are used as infrequently as six times a year. In a house, the bedroom is likely to be situated on an upper floor and therefore blessed with good natural light, inspiring views and separation from general family noise and disturbance. This can be the absolutely ideal environment; it is self-contained and the door can be closed at the end of the working day.

Before office plans are drawn up, take time to consider the design, space-planning and décor. Can the room be designated solely as an office or does it need to occasionally double as a guest room? Think about how the room might function. Should it work like a bedroom with an office in the corner, or is it to be an office with a bed in the corner? The decision depends on the type of work undertaken and how frequently guests visit.

LEFT *A minimal workstation in a converted attic bedroom has the benefits of being well lit by the rooflight and peaceful during the day. Although this work area is intended only for part-time use, it has been thoughtfully designed with a long, trestle-style table to complement the horizontal lines of the room.*

OPPOSITE *This office shares its space with the living room. The bespoke, built-in unit functions well for those who need little desk space. The door to the cupboard where the office equipment is stored acts as a desktop when pulled down. When no longer required, it is closed up.*

Many of these workstations are compact, most have doors, so that the whole unit can be closed up at the end of the working day, and some are fitted with casters so they can be wheeled out of the way when they are not being used.

If your working life is likely to be too complex to be accommodated in such a unit, an increasing number of furniture manufacturers are now selling modular systems, which can be fitted together to make a built-in office. Based closely on the fitted kitchen, the units are often promoted for awkward spaces such as under the stairs, in hallways or even in part of the attic. Like kitchen cabinets, built-in

ABOVE *An unusual work pavilion has been built at the heart of this living space. It wraps round a structural column and is screened from the living area by walls at not quite ceiling height. This design device reduces the structure's impact on the room by allowing light to flow over the top of the office.*

RIGHT *A tailor-made solution includes suitable shelving for files, a horizontal rack for stationery, a pin board and retractable keyboard tray.*

OPPOSITE *Redundant space at the turn of the stair has been transformed into a neat office featuring a built-in solid slab desktop, which spans the space between two walls.*

If there is no spare bedroom, a more creative solution will be needed to accommodate the home office. Part-time and occasional workers may well be satisfied with sharing another room; the kitchen or living room are favourites. If only a small space is required, perhaps just a desk with drawers will suffice. Don't get carried away thinking that you would like vast amounts of storage, desk space and shelf space if you really only need something quite minimal. If a desk is too modest, then an all-in-one, office-in-a-box workstation might be just right. These clever designs are specifically for home use and have helpful features such as a phone shelf, space for a large computer, built-in file drawers and cable management, to prevent computer, printer and telephone cables trailing around the house.

office units are often extremely ingenious in offering plenty of very useful storage options, and they do provide a means of marking the boundary of the home office. However, on the downside, they often score badly when it comes to aesthetics.

Other ideas for dual-use spaces include wide hallways and landings. Here you may miss out on good quality natural light, and will need to work under artificial light, but there may be excellent space gains. For example, you could set up a long worktop with plenty of room above and below for storage. Corridors also offer the opportunity for huge amounts of storage space: a wall lined with shelving and fronted by floor-to-ceiling hinged or sliding doors will give copious storage potential and provide strict boundaries for office material.

For those who work full time and have decided that they deserve the biggest and best possible quality of workspace, a dedicated office is a must. This decision will almost certainly involve spending money converting existing underused space such as an attic, basement or garage, or perhaps even building on an extension. My advice is that if you are serious about your work at home, you should be serious about your workspace, and money spent improving the work environment is money well spent. It is worth noting that not only will the creation of an extra office room save money otherwise diverted to renting offices, but it should also add value and sales appeal to your home. In recent housing surveys, a significant majority of respondents said that a high priority for them when property hunting is a home with a ready-made office space, or at least the potential for an office.

Space under the stairs is often given over to storage, and, in this case, a home office fits perfectly under the flight of metal stairs and the unusual mezzanine that floats overhead. It is a simple arrangement: a couple of desks and wall-fixed adjustable shelving. The industrial style of the office matches that of the apartment.

practicalities

ABOVE *Basements can make interesting, if challenging, home offices. There are few distractions and the soundproofing is good, but lighting can pose a problem. Here, a large window draws in light from the garden, but additional artificial lighting is needed over the desk area.*

OPPOSITE *A mezzanine area, with the advantages of being light and away from the main living area, has been converted into an office.*

Interestingly, it is also the case that a number of smart housebuilders in both the US and Europe are now including an office in their designs.

The attic or basement can make a good, even excellent workspace, but both often require an energetic imagination and a healthy budget to realize their full potential. Attics can provide valuable peace and quiet and a high degree of separation from everyday home life, and, with the inclusion of large rooflights, they are usually well lit. But be sure there will be adequate headroom; no one wants to end up with a permanent stoop or crick in the neck. Most older homes do have a good roof height, but there are drawbacks to modern houses where roof

levels may be lower and roof structures do not allow for conversion unless large amounts of money are spent altering and bracing the existing struts. The main disadvantage of basing a home office in an attic becomes apparent when large numbers of visitors are expected: it can be awkward making clients walk through the entire house and up several flights of stairs for meetings.

At the other extreme, ceiling height and natural light are the main considerations when planning a basement conversion. If the ceiling height is limited, it may be an expensive excavation operation to dig out additional height. However, it is always worth asking a builder to quote, because you may find that the work is easily accomplished. When it comes to maximizing light in a basement, architects often devise amazingly inventive solutions. Clever design tricks include excavating out into the garden to make a lightwell addition to the basement. If it is impossible to have natural light in the area, I would forget about it as a viable workspace. After all, can there possibly be anything more depressing and counterproductive than being hidden away in a windowless space and trying to work? Alternative options here might involve relocating a bathroom to the basement, a bedroom even, and then moving the office into the freed-up space.

The garage conversion can be a neat job, too, providing extensive office space. But if you have to use the garage for the car, perhaps you can build a room above it? Adding on rooms for offices allows you to make a space just as you choose and even create a separate entrance. This may increase the vulnerability of your office to burglars, but visitors are not exposed to your home life.

Finally, there is the humble garden shed: for those with a garden, a completely separate outdoor pavilion – direct from the garden centre or architect-designed – could be a haven for homeworkers. The costs can be relatively low, the space can be designed precisely to meet your needs, a clear distinction is made between home and work, and you could have a truly inspiring environment. But there are downsides, too. For example, you may need to apply for planning permission; heating and lighting will need to be laid on; and money spent on a work shed may not add as much to the value of your home as a permanent extension.

furniture and equipment

Choosing the best furniture and equipment for your home office will ensure that you are able to carry out a normal day's work seated at your desk without suffering any pain or discomfort. If you do experience any persistent muscular pain, or even if your muscles just feel stiff occasionally, it is almost certain that something is wrong. You may be able to relieve the symptoms by altering your work habits, such as building in more breaks, but most sensible of all, is to make sure you have the right furniture in the first place.

Among the most important purchases you will make when setting up a home office are the desk and chair. For years employers have recognized the good sense in keeping employees comfortable, to ensure that they work to their full potential. Exactly the same logic applies to working at home. Often,

out of necessity, people setting up their offices at home do so on limited budgets, but the desk and chair are most definitely no place to cut corners.

The study of ergonomics has helped us to understand how our bodies perform in the work environment, and how we are able to work more efficiently when the stresses of discomfort are reduced or removed. Around the globe there is now strict legislation to ensure that minimum standards for office health and safety are met. But if you are self-employed, the responsibility for your wellbeing is obviously yours. When a workstation is well designed it can help prevent bodily damage caused by strain in such sensitive areas as the back, arms and hands. Good design is therefore essential for comfort, health, job satisfaction, motivation and a sense of accomplishment.

are you sitting comfortably?

It is easy to get into the habit of sitting badly and ignoring the warning signals given by your body when it is suffering from a bad posture. These guidelines will help ensure you are sitting at your desk in a way that should prevent aches and pains.

MAKE SURE your body, particularly your spine, feels well supported by the chair.

FEET should rest flat on the floor.

SHOULDERS should be in a relaxed, neutral position and not hunched or bent forward.

KNEES should fit comfortably under the desk.

KEYBOARD should be within easy reach and, when typing, your wrists should not be bent upwards.

DO NOT grip the mouse too tightly as this will cause muscle strain.

KEEP TOOLS in regular hourly or daily use within easy reaching distance from your chair.

IF YOU USE the telephone for prolonged periods, consider investing in a telephonist's headset.

IF YOU OFTEN need to type from books and documents, think about buying a document rest to prop up the material and hold it in a comfortable reading position.

OPPOSITE *For the sake of your health and general comfort, a well-designed desk and chair are essential. Invest time researching and trying out a number of chairs, look at the different desk configurations on the market, and be prepared to pay for the best possible quality. It will be money spent wisely.*

the chair

The best office design begins with the needs of the individual. And so the most important piece of equipment in any home office has to be the chair. People working full time can expect to be at their desks for at least six or seven hours a day. Research has shown that homeworkers are likely to put in longer hours than their office counterparts and, with fewer distractions from colleagues, it is usual for them to work in a more concentrated way. Be wary of falling into the trap of sitting for hours on end without getting up and moving around. Build in rests and excuses for standing, taking a break, spending an hour at the gym or going for a walk.

The best chairs are, unsurprisingly, expensive, but in setting up a home office you have the opportunity and luxury of choosing a chair that is right for you and the way you work. A good chair might cost almost as much as a computer, but it is always money worth spending. Good health and high productivity depend on being seated properly; without them you cannot hope to earn a living.

Any office set-up budget will include a large slice of cash for vital equipment, such as a state-of-the-art computer. But, if you have the choice, I would suggest trimming a little off the computer budget – extra computer capacity can always be installed later – and transferring it to what you spend on the chair. If you choose not to invest in a good chair and opt to sit at an ordinary dining chair, you will soon discover that the hard seat provides only minimal support. Ergonomic research has shown that by sitting on a hard chair, pressure on the lumbar discs is increased by as much as 30 per cent; in plain English, there is no better way of storing up back trouble. The cost and time spent visiting an osteopath is better invested at the outset in a well-designed chair.

Although in recent years there has been a multimillion dollar worldwide investment into the research and design of the perfect office chair, there

is still no consensus on all the elements. However, there is agreement on the basics: a good chair must provide comfort and support. The ideal would be a chair made to fit the body exactly, to match the height and weight of the user and with a range of working positions. The closest that manufacturers have come to this ideal is the fully adjustable model. Most ergonomists recommend them highly because they provide support while also offering plenty of sitting options. No one sits in the same position for an entire day; in fact most of us hold positions for no longer than a few minutes before crossing legs or shifting to a slightly different position.

Take note of how you sit at your desk when working and select a chair that offers the most appropriate seating option. There are three main styles of sitting when working: leaning forward is the commonest position for those who spend a lot of their time writing, drawing or looking through research material; sitting upright is usual for people who do a lot of keying-in on their computers; and backward leaning is the style most often adopted by

choosing a chair

SET ASIDE as generous a budget as possible.

LOOK FOR A CHAIR that fits your body; if you have short legs, you will not need a deep seat, and make sure the backrest supports you in the right places.

OPT FOR ADJUSTABLE FEATURES to cope with your posture and how you sit while working.

CHECK THE UPHOLSTERY: the chair should be firm and comfortable.

TRY OUT plenty of chairs to decide which style of backrest you prefer.

CHOOSE A CHAIR with well-padded but detachable armrests.

MAKE SURE the armrests are adjustable or that they are set at a height where they will not crash into your desk worktop.

CONSIDER CAREFULLY whether you prefer fixed legs or casters.

Ergonomic design is invaluable. The body is subjected to a huge range of stresses during the course of an average working day and a well-designed chair is essential. This state-of-the-art chair has an adjustable back and seat, and the armrests can be set at different heights or removed altogether.

those who talk a great deal on the phone. For people who perform a variety of tasks, the seating positions will be a mixture of all three styles.

When trying out chairs – and I would strongly recommend that you visit at least three showrooms to gauge exactly what is available – make sure that your bottom fits deep into the seat and that your feet can still rest flat and comfortably on the floor, with your knees forming a 90-degree angle. The seat should be padded and firm and provide support under the thighs, but there should be little or no upward pressure pushing your knees above pelvis height. If the padding is too thin or too rigid, there is the danger of cutting off or reducing the blood supply to the lower leg, which will cause poor circulation and numbness.

Office chairs have different types of height adjustment, most of which are based on hydraulics. Some adjust to your weight each time you sit down, while others can be set and locked at a comfortable height. I would suggest choosing a chair that has the option of locking the height and backrest in positions that suit you best.

If the sitting position and height of the chair feel comfortable, make sure that your back is well supported. Most advice suggests that the lower back or lumbar region is the area demanding most care and attention. Find a chair that does not dig in to your back but which hugs the curve of your spine

Sit back, relax and enjoy your work. Here is a glimpse of the future with a body-hugging chair designed to give support exactly where it is needed: the head, neck, lower back and elbows. It is particularly effective when used with voice-activated technology.

and gives a firm backrest. The question of whether this back support is fixed or allows a certain degree of rocking is usually considered a matter of taste. If you move back and forth a lot while working, you will probably become incredibly irritated to find your movement shadowed by the chairback. However, some users find this style of chair very comfortable. If you sit at your desk for long periods of time, you might find a degree of backrest movement welcome as the rocking motion is known to relieve muscle strain. It is also considered beneficial to the spine and circulation – even the digestion. My preferred type of backrest is the sort that holds the back in an upright position but which can also be moved further back by pushing against the back pad. It has a soft-lock that is released with pressure.

Simple typist's chairs can give good support for working in short bursts. For long periods of concentrated computer work, a more supportive, adjustable chair is recommended.

With chairs where the backrest does move, many ergonomists also suggest that the seat should tilt gently to match the back movement and provide full body support. Some of the newest chairs on the market are so cleverly articulated that they offer an almost completely reclined position. The design is actually inspired by voice-activated technology; when workers no longer need to be crouched over a keyboard, they can lie back and talk to computers.

Then there are the details: do you want a chair with armrests and should you choose fixed legs or wheels? My advice is always to buy a chair with removable, well-padded armrests. If they feel good, keep them; if they don't, you always have the option of taking them off. I would also suggest that wheels are preferable to fixed legs because they make the chair easier to move around. But a word of caution about them: it is not a good idea to 'scoot' around your office on the chair because this jarring action is very tough on the body, particularly the spine. If you need to cross the room, it is better to stand up and walk.

Almost all new office chairs have a star-shaped base with five feet. This design provides maximum stability – it is almost impossible to topple over. If your budget will not stretch to a new chair and you have to buy a secondhand one, avoid those with only four feet, which are notoriously unstable.

A solid and comfortable looking chair with a backrest to keep the spine in its natural 'S' shape. There is divided opinion between those who prefer fixed feet on their chairs and those who favour casters. Casters allow easy movement, but can encourage 'scooting' around the floor, which puts incredible pressure on the back muscles.

the desk

Choosing a desk is also an opportunity to make your home office fit you and the way you work. Traditionally, a big desk had to be earned; it was a status symbol and had little or nothing to do with practicality but, fortunately, that is no longer the case. I would recommend buying the largest possible worksurface that will fit the space because it is comforting to know that you can always extend your working area should you need to. It can be a big mistake, and intensely irritating, to try to fit your working life on to a desk that is far too small. However, the choice of worktop size does depend on the work to be undertaken. There are a small number of occupations that entail using just a laptop computer and phone, in which case a vast runway-sized desk would be excessive.

The desk should be strong and rigid, providing a worksurface that is large enough to accommodate everyday work equipment and accessories (see chart below). If you have a computer, you need to be able to position the computer and keyboard directly in front of you, with the monitor at a comfortable distance from your eyes – usually around 60cm (2ft). With this in mind, a useful desktop depth should probably be no less than 90cm (3ft), and the length no less than 1.4m (4½ft). The colour and finish of

calculating the desktop area

This sample calculation shows how to calculate the optimum worksurface area so that you have plenty of space for organizing tools as well as a useful working area. List all the equipment and tools in regular use, including small items, such as a mousemat and desk diary, then measure their 'footprint' – the space they occupy – and double the total.

Computer, including space for wiring	45x35cm (18x14in)	= 1575sq cm (252sq in)
Mousemat	25x20cm (10x8in)	= 500sq cm (80sq in)
Phone/answering machine	20x25cm (8x10in)	= 500sq cm (80sq in)
Modem	15x20cm (6x8in)	= 300sq cm (48sq in)
Desk diary (open)	30x30cm (12x12in)	= 900sq cm (144sq in)
Pen holder	15x15cm (6x6in)	= 225sq cm (36sq in)
Notebook (open)	50x30cm (20x12in)	= 1500sq cm (240sq in)
In-tray	30x40cm (12x16in)	= 1200sq cm (192sq in)
Desk lamp	15x15cm (6x6in)	= 225sq cm (36sq in)
Coffee mat	13x13cm (5x5in)	= 169sq cm (25sq in)
Paperweight	8x8cm (3x3in)	= 64sq cm (9sq in)
TOTAL		= 7158sq cm (1142sq in)

By doubling this figure, you have a total of 14316sq cm (2284sq in), which gives you a worksurface area of approximately 1x1.5m (3x5ft).

the worktop are important, too. Soft colours, such as mid-grey, are kinder on the eye, unlike deeply contrasting colours, such as black and white. Glossy surfaces can cause eyestrain and create unwelcome reflections; a soft matt finish is preferable.

The worktop height is usually the same as the elbow height of the user when seated. To check this, measure the desktop height while you are seated in a comfortable position. You should be able to sit at the worktop in a relaxed position, without hunching up your shoulders (if you do, the desk is too high), and without your shoulders sloping forward (if you do, the desk is too low). Buying a desk of the right height will help to make working as comfortable as possible while also preventing muscle stress and physical distortion.

If there is a generous space available for your desk, consider different configurations. A worktop running the length of a wall can produce a really satisfying horizontal line as well as providing a useful working and storage area. An L-shape desk fitting

ABOVE *An unusual desk with a generous worktop area and built-in storage at either end. The shallow shelf below the worktop is designed to hold large sheets of paper.*

OPPOSITE *The ultimate in minimal desktops – a counter spanning the space between the walls – demonstrates that if this is all you need, you do not have to spend a fortune on office furniture.*

choosing a desk

SELECT the largest worksurface you can, and no smaller than 1x1.5m (3x5ft), unless you are one of the few workers who needs the minimum of equipment such as a laptop and phone.

MAKE SURE the desk is solid and rigid.

AVOID strong-coloured and reflective worksurfaces.

AIM FOR a height that is around the level of your elbow when seated.

IF YOU SPEND a lot of the time at the keyboard, think about a lower-level keyboard tray, which might be more comfortable.

CONSIDER THE LAYOUT PLAN: is there room for an L-shape or U-shape desk arrangement?

IN MOST CASES desk drawers are an asset, but make sure there is still plenty of legroom.

A DESK with built-in channels for electrical cabling is highly recommended.

into a corner can create a deep triangular recess to accommodate a large computer and two 'wings' for non-computer-related tasks. A U-shape is another option and one that gives the user plenty of surface area and above-desk shelf space within easy reach while remaining seated.

Desks can provide very useful storage space. Deep filing drawers that accommodate hanging files make everyday paperwork easily accessible. Small drawers are invaluable for those items that inevitably make up the necessary collection of work tools, such as staplers, paper punches, marker pens, ink cartridges, transparency viewers, paperclips, and so on. Many desks also feature built-in cable channels. Some sort of cable management is highly desirable when setting up a desk with a range of electrical equipment – computer, modem, lamp, telephone and mobile phone – because it not only protects the cabling, but it is also aesthetically pleasing to tidy away all those wires.

ABOVE An unusual elliptical desk with a neat drawer unit fitted underneath. The worktop is finished in a soft matt pewter grey – a soothing background colour.

RIGHT An ingenious piece of design, the desk is cantilevered from the wall and contains three slim drawers, two of which spin out to provide extra worktop space when needed. The shelving above, also made of blond plywood, echoes the dimensions of the desktop.

OPPOSITE In this dual-use home office, the mobile desk sits on a small, raised platform to separate it from the sleeping area. The compact all-in-one unit has just enough space for a computer and keyboard and a small amount of storage.

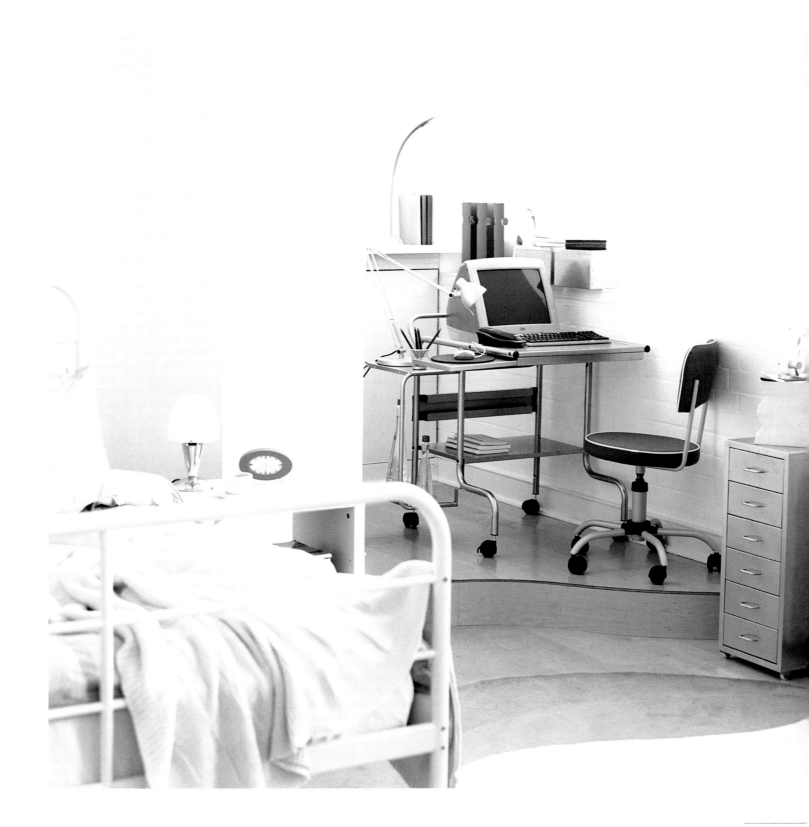

worktop layout

With the right chair and the right desk, the home office is already taking shape. The next step is to arrange work tools, reference material, files, reports and any other equipment in a way that makes work easier and more comfortable.

The worktop plan begins with the computer. All ergonomic experts and office designers agree that the best position for the computer monitor is directly in front of the user (see page 45). However, opinion is divided about the best height for the monitor. In Europe, the norm is to keep the monitor on the desk, making the top of the screen at about the same height as the eyes. However, there is a body of opinion, mostly in the US, that believes the monitor should be placed lower, sunk into the desktop, so that the eyes look down at the monitor.

There are also differences of opinion about the ideal height for the keyboard. In Europe it is usually placed on the worktop, while, in the US, there is a growing belief that it should be a few inches lower, to reduce muscle strain and give free wrist movement during typing. I would suggest trying out both options to see which feels most comfortable. I can see the good sense of having the keyboard at a lower level than the desktop, but having tried several systems, it does seem much less convenient than having everything on the same desktop. If the keyboard is placed on a pull-out tray, it interrupts access to the rest of the worktop, making everyday tasks like using the phone difficult. On balance, I keep my keyboard on the desktop, but if I had to do a lot more typing, I would consider a stowable, pull-out tray.

Once you have the computer in place, all the other tools and materials in regular use should be arranged within easy reach in an arc around you — that means an arm's reach involving little or no stretching and body twisting. The arc can take in the area around the body from chair seat height to chin height. Those who conduct most of their business on the phone will find it most comfortable if the handset is well within arm's reach, just beside the

Two self-contained workstations, with the monitors placed directly in front of the users, retractable keyboard shelves, computer tower on the floor and bespoke shelving.

computer. It might even be a good idea to invest in a hands-free telephonist's headset, to make note-taking easier. Placing the phone just a few inches further away can make a tremendous difference, as that extra stretch to reach it could be responsible for back and neck aches.

Do make sure that there is enough room on the worktop for writing notes, and that means there must also be space for stowing or moving aside the keyboard. Another option is to keep part of the worktop permanently for computer use and part of it for making phone calls.

Think about other items that you use on a daily basis, such as a stapler, paper punch, marker pens, and sticky tape, and work out ways of storing them close to the work hub. A small hanging shelf unit is a good idea and brings order where there might otherwise be chaos. Reference material – diary, dictionaries, price lists, ledgers, and so on – is also

positioning your computer, keyboard and mouse

This sounds like the easiest thing in the world, but it is astounding how many people do not get it right. All too often the computer monitor is shoved to one side of the desk, which makes it awkward to use and will almost certainly cause muscle contortion and strain in the neck, shoulders and back.

FOR ANYONE who spends most of their working life using a computer, the monitor must be set up directly in front of the body.

WHEN YOU ARE IN a comfortable seating position for working, the monitor screen should be at arm's length from you – approximately 60cm (2ft).

THE HEIGHT AND ANGLE of the monitor is a subject for debate, but most experts agree that the top of the screen should be at, or below, eye level and angled backwards, with the top of the screen further away from you than the bottom.

PLACE THE KEYBOARD directly in front of the monitor with the mouse to one side.

A slightly cramped set-up, but the elements are all in the right place for this worker. The monitor and keyboard are directly in front of the user, a document holder sits to one side and is illuminated with the task light, and the frequently used fax machine is within arm's reach.

This is a ready-made desk intended for those whose work is primarily computer based. There is little room for laying out documents, but it is a sturdy unit with a neat, retractable keyboard shelf. The open shelving at the side provides useful storage for items needed on a regular basis, plus a mini sound system.

best stored close to the desk. If there is a lot of this material, including files that are updated or checked regularly, it is a good idea to add a shelf unit perpendicular to the desk. Items in less frequent use – a mobile phone charger unit, perhaps – can be placed right on the edge of the desk, or even on a shelf away from the immediate desk area.

While it makes good sense to keep regularly used items within arm's reach, it is also important to build in excuses to get up from your seat, to stand and cross the room and stretch your muscles (see also pages 154–5). Those items used perhaps only once or twice a day can be stored on a shelf or in a file further from the desk.

This pair of desks makes a great expanse of worktop. The wall is used as a pinboard, and desk-height shelves house small items such as CDs. The computers sit to one side on the desktop as they are not in constant use, while the phones are easily accessible. Because this is a graphic design-based business, the generous worktop allows paperwork to be spread out flat, and the all-important felt-tipped pens, which are used throughout the day, are within easy reach.

recycling materials

Despite decades of talk about the paperless office, paper remains the main business medium. Although there is much debate about the rights and wrongs of paper recycling, for those who opt for recycled paper there is now a vast range of high-quality material to choose from for every office use.

Good office practice includes using both sides of a sheet of paper for making notes. Convert old reports into scrap pads, buy re-use labels to stick on recycled envelopes. You probably would not want to send them to your most important clients, but they do have many other uses, such as organizing random reports and documents.

There are all sorts of opportunities for recycling, such as re-using files, ring binders and refillable pens. Some companies operate schemes where it is possible to have spent laser and inkjet cartridges collected free for recycling. They are filled and sold back at a lower-than-new price. Where possible, always recycle and repair instead of throwing away.

When it comes to office waste, the best advice is to do what the Americans and Scandinavians do: sort materials into separate bags for plastics, metals, glass and paper. It requires commitment and time, but it is the only viable way to recycle. Take the collected material to your nearest recycling centre or look in a local telephone directory to find a waste collecting and recycling operator.

Finally, check with your supplier when buying almost anything, from a keyboard to a kettle, that broken parts can be easily replaced and whether the item is made of a recyclable material.

thinking green and keeping down costs

Inevitably working at home will increase your home-running expenses, but there are a number of measures that you can take to help save money. In reducing your energy costs, you will also do your bit for the environment. You should also be able to offset a portion of your heating and lighting bills against tax.

ADJUST your timer control to ensure the central heating is turned on only when it is required.

ADD draughtproof strips to windows and doors.

TURN OFF lights when not needed.

REPLACE your most-used regular lightbulbs with low-energy ones.

CHECK the energy-efficiency credentials of any new electrical appliance you buy, especially a computer.

DON'T switch on your computer first thing in the morning if you are not likely to use it until after lunch, and always remember to switch it off when you finish work.

DON'T leave electrical equipment on standby; it still consumes energy.

LOCATE companies who offer ink and toner cartridge refilling.

USE the unprinted side of documents for scrap paper to make into note pads.

OPPOSITE *A simple but effective set-up where office paper and magazines are saved in one square bin and collected for recycling. The second square bin is used to collect paper suitable for making into note pads and for sketching. The small circular bin is for actual waste.*

Closed storage units such as this wooden chest and box-file shelving keep down dust levels. The plastic Venetian blinds and bare floorboards also help to make cleaning easy.

For those who suffer from asthma and allergies, the home office is full of potential distress. Chemically treated upholstery fabrics and carpets, solvent-based paints, varnishes and printing inks, plastics, such as computer casing material, poor ventilation and moulds exacerbated by double glazing and harsh cleaning materials all conspire to cause allergy attacks. The clear message is that simple is safest. Try to avoid materials such as modern synthetic carpets and upholstery fabrics that have probably been heavily treated with chemicals.

One of the most commonly identified enemies of the acute allergy sufferer is the house dust mite or, more accurately, its droppings. Invisible to the naked eye, this microscopic monster likes nothing better than damp and warm crevices, particularly in carpets, fabrics and furniture, where it feeds on human skin scales. So, instead of curtains, fit blinds, and use plain, unbleached cottons for cushions, rugs and upholstery. These simple fabrics can be washed regularly to keep away dust as well as mites. Instead of carpeting, opt for bare boards or linoleum, and clean regularly with a filter vacuum.

Keep dust traps to a minimum: avoid fabric lampshades and framed pictures, which may collect dust around the frame. To keep the air really crisp, try small electrical air filters and purifiers.

Since dust is such a powerful irritant to allergy sufferers, those with the most serious problems tend to use cupboards or glass-fronted shelving for all their office storage as this reduces the amount of dust building up on shelves. Those who are affected by the printing inks used in books, magazines and newspapers should store them in a utility room or a cupboard in another room, until the strong-smelling volatile chemicals have dispersed.

When it comes to decorating, wallpaper is not an option because it collects dust and harbours moulds that grow between the paper and the plaster. Traditional wall coatings, such as distemper, may be among the most suitable since they are made simply of chalk, natural pigment, water and a natural sizing agent, which stabilizes the surface. There are also low-odour versions of modern petro-chemical emulsions and gloss paints available.

Secondhand furniture is popular with allergy sufferers and asthmatics because any distressing vapours from paints or stains are likely to have already evaporated. If you are buying new furniture,

opt for natural, untreated woods, which can be left plain or coloured with water-based and low-allergy stainers or paints. Avoid furniture that has been made from modern materials such as MDF, which is composed of tiny particles suspended in a plastic resin. Although these should not cause any irritation when they are properly sealed, the particles can actually be released into the atmosphere if the material becomes damaged or scratched.

Many acute allergy sufferers find computers difficult to cope with because of the plastic vapours they emit, which irritate the eyes, throat and skin; older computers tend to be less of a problem. Switch on your computer only when it is needed, to reduce the volume of irritants released into the air, and cover it with a scarf or cloth at other times. If at all possible, keep fax machines and photocopiers, which also emit irritants, in a separate room.

A pristine space with easily cleaned surfaces, including the tiled floor. Carpets, which harbour dust and are often treated with petro-chemical sprays, should be avoided by the allergy sufferer. Although plants trap dust on their leaves, wiping with a damp cloth will keep the plant and the homeworker happy.

storage

Thoughtfully planned, well-organized

storage space is the key to an efficient,

smooth-running office

storage overview

When planning and designing storage solutions, the aims are manifold. They include being able to create order where there is the threat of chaos, to design a logical plan, to be able to find anything quickly and to introduce some hierarchy for those items in regular use as well as those needed infrequently. Ergonomic planning, providing safe storage for vulnerable items and stopping home-office spread by building in the facility to identify and clear out unwanted material at regular intervals should also be considered. Any storage design should attempt to answer all or most of these requirements.

At the start of the design process, remember that there is a universal law applying to all storage solutions: no matter how much room you have, it will never seem to be enough. Creating sufficient storage is a tough design challenge, and in recent years, space organization has become a discipline in its own right: many companies are dedicated solely to providing and manufacturing storage solutions, ranging from the compact, well-ordered wardrobe to the home office built into the attic. The designers all share the same goal, that of maximum capacity with maximum efficiency.

In most home offices there is a huge volume of paper-based support material that must be ordered and managed. When done well, it is an invaluable asset to the smooth running of the working day. Where there is control over reference books, files, reports, there is control over the whole work process, which inevitably has a positive effect on the finished result. There are few things more infuriating than spending hours looking for something that you know you saw just the day before.

An organizer's dream. This home
office has fitted cupboards, drawers
and shelves covering almost every
scrap of wall surface, right up to
the apex of the roof. The units are
exquisite showpieces of modern
cabinetmaking, the blond wood
offset by brushed stainless steel
handles. The materials re-appear
in the elegant, trestle-style desk.

assessing your storage

A range of freestanding storage solutions has been incorporated in this space, from the old-fashioned wooden filing cabinet and compact chest of tiny, square drawers to the stack of see-through plastic boxes on the floor. Even the simple desk has its own built-in storage space in slim shelves under the worktop.

In choosing and planning your office storage, it is a good idea to start by identifying the type of material to be stored – that is, everything not kept on the desktop. Think about the range of storage options. Do you need shelving as well as cupboard space? Is most of your stored paperwork an archive that is accessed infrequently? Do you have heavy items or lots of small items? And then there are questions of style. Do you prefer an office-interior look or would domestic-style furniture be more appropriate? If the workspace is in a shared room, such as a guest bedroom or living area, are you happy that your work is permanently on display or would you prefer to be able to screen it off in some way? Where at all possible, avoid drab and make-do options; your working environment could be considered one of the most important spaces you inhabit and, like everything else, storage should be designed to feel interesting, uplifting and inviting.

Anyone who has ever moved offices will have an idea of the enormous volume of material it takes to support everyday working life. It hardly seems

LEFT *Many professions are a magnet for books, and the neat solution to contain so many volumes is a built-in cabinet that makes the most of floor-to-ceiling wall space. The swivel door is a wonderful reinterpretation of secret library doors found in grand country homes of the 18th and 19th centuries.*

BELOW *An unusual and decorative storage unit composed of staggered wooden cubes. Although the cubes appear to be stacked randomly, they are, in fact, cleverly held in place by a stainless steel pole threaded through the back of them.*

credible that a desk and a few shelves of books and files could occupy perhaps seven or eight removal crates. For those working at home, the volume is likely to be even greater since the office has to contain an entire one-person business with accounts books, archive and reference library. Always make estimates generous and leave room for growth.

As you make your list of materials requiring storage, estimate how much space they will take up. Even apparently insignificant small-scale items, such as computer disks, will need to be kept somewhere. In addition, make a note of those items you use regularly, those you need perhaps only weekly or monthly, and those you may need to access only rarely. The distinction drawn between different types of material helps in assessing where it is stored: for example, past accounting books and files can be classed as archive material and, if space is limited, stored outside the office in a secure garage, for example (see also pages 72–3).

In building a clear picture of the contents of your home office, different storage options will start to emerge. While books are most readily accessed on open shelves, files may be too cumbersome to fit on the same unit and might be better off with their own dedicated space with deeper shelving. Large numbers of small items can look interesting, even decorative, gathered together on open shelves or in glass-fronted cupboards. If you would prefer not to see all your work-related material on display, choose a solid-fronted cupboard. If you have expensive technical equipment, such as cameras and recording machines, or precious and hazardous materials, the best option may be to store them in a lockable, fireproof, mice-proof cupboard, while a safe would be desirable for valuable goods and cash. Any office is likely to have contents that fit into a number of very different categories.

OPPOSITE *Look for extra pockets of space and you should find some. Here, the dead area at the top of the staircase has been put to good use as a small, remote-storage library. It is reached by a flight of glass-tread stairs, which allow light from the rooflight to cascade down the stairwell.*

calculating storage space

Whether opting for built-in or freestanding storage, it is helpful to roughly measure all the materials you plan to store at the outset, to gauge just how much space you are likely to need, and what kind of storage will be the most suitable. This sample calculation for a journalist should provide a useful starting point for working out your own storage requirements. It is a universal law that you will always need more storage than you expect, so build in room to grow. Of course, the growth rate will depend on the type of work being undertaken, but as a rough guide I would suggest adding an extra 25 per cent to your totals.

ITEM TO BE STORED	APPROX LENGTH	APPROX HEIGHT	STORAGE OPTION
Reference books, manuals, directories	30m (100ft)	35cm (14in)	shelving
Small size books	2m (6½ft)	20cm (8in)	shelving
Magazines, brochures, catalogues	5m (16ft)	40cm (16in)	shelving
Box and book files	4m (13ft)	45cm (18in)	shelving
Hanging files	3m (10ft)	30cm (12in)	filing cabinet
Accounts material	1.5m (5ft)	45cm (18in)	shelving/ cupboard
Stationery: paper, envelopes, pens	1m (3ft)	30cm (12in)	shelving/ cupboard
Everyday work tools	1m (3ft)	40cm (16in)	desktop/ shelving
Radio/hi-fi system	50cm (1½ft)	50cm (20in)	shelving
Television/video	60cm (2ft)	60cm (24in)	shelving/cupboard
Archive material	3m (10ft)	50cm (20in)	cupboard in office/remote storage

built-in or freestanding?

Making the choice between built-in or freestanding storage units for the home office is, in the end, a matter of taste and space, and perhaps also budget. As a general rule, built-in shelving and cupboards tend to make much better use of the available space than freestanding units. However, the advantage of freestanding items is that they are portable and more likely to be easily integrated into the domestic environment. Interestingly, many office furniture manufacturers are taking the best from both worlds and producing systems that include a mixture of built-in and freestanding items.

Freestanding units are particularly useful in small and temporary offices where there is only a low volume of material to be stored. Items such as open shelves help to keep an airy feel in a restricted space. Another advantage of freestanding units is that they are easily moved around the room, and from home to home.

storage

Just like the fitted kitchen, a modular office system should make the most of awkward spaces and, at the same time, provide a neat solution in shared-use rooms, where a fitted workstation will contain the potential spread of all work-related material. There are dozens of styles of off-the-peg storage systems on the market, from the traditional-looking wood finishes to the most striking steel and glass units. It is advisable to choose a system that will not only look good for years, but that will also be available in the future, should you ever need to expand. If you have a lavish budget or a particularly awkward space to work with, a bespoke fitted office opens up the opportunity to create something really individual, giving you the choice of materials and style of units as well as making sure that the office is tailor-made precisely to suit your needs.

Freestanding units, on the other hand, offer a degree of flexibility that is not achievable with built-in shelving and cupboards. Among the available options are bookcases, filing cabinets, room dividers and worktables, as well as more specialized items such as the architect's plan chest and the slimmest book shelf ideal for slotting into an underused corner. All of these can be moved easily around the room, and be taken with you if you move house.

Whatever your preferred style of design – contemporary and colourful or more clubby and traditional – there are freestanding units available, which discreetly become part of the furniture. Depending on the look you are aiming to achieve, it is possible to reduce the office's visual impact on a shared room by keeping storage items at or below worktop level, and in cupboards rather than on open shelves. If you would like to have the office contained in a small portion of the room, why not consider building vertically? A floor-to-ceiling unit will have enormous storage capacity, and if you do not want a constant reminder of the office, fit solid cupboard doors, even a blind or curtain, to cover everything. Alternatively, you may want to celebrate the office look by making a feature of potentially

ABOVE TOP AND BELOW
Now you see it, now you don't. Flush-fit doors are a classic design device for reducing visual intrusion in a space. When the doors of this unit are closed the space is calm and streamlined; when open, it demonstrates just how much can be accommodated in built-in cupboards, drawers and shelves.

ABOVE *Industrial-style metal shelving looks smart in this contemporary interior. The open unit has a central spine of upright posts fixed to floor and ceiling, from which shelves are hung either side. Not only can the shelving take books of varying sizes, it also acts as a subtle space divider.*

RIGHT *A sliding 'wall' on runners opens to reveal a floor-to-ceiling library of built-in shelving. When the partition is pulled across, it allows the homeworker to quickly shut off from work at the end of the day.*

BELOW *A salvage-style filing cabinet adds character to this cool, stripped-back office. The cabinet has a large drawer for hanging files and two smaller drawers for stationery. Fitted with casters, it is easy to move around the space or to clear out of the way when not in use.*

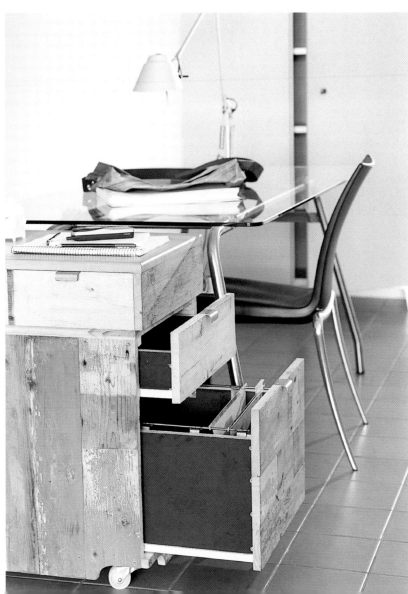

This double-act of a room divider
provides storage space in the home
office as well as the living area.
On the office side of the unit there
is space for filing, and on the
other side book shelves. When not
required, and to open up the space,
the whole case can simply be
wheeled to another location.

boring items, for example, files: choose all the same colour, or alternate black and white, and display them neatly on open shelves.

Another great advantage of these individual freestanding items is their versatility. It is easy to assemble an office quickly from unfitted units, which is ideal if you need to create work space for just a short time, perhaps for a one-off project or if you are working temporarily in one room while waiting for an extension to be built. When it is time to move, packing up and moving are relatively

straightforward. The virtue of flexibility also means that if you are not completely happy with your office arrangement, it can be changed quickly and with relatively little disruption.

The variety of freestanding units available on the market is vast, but perhaps the most useful and ubiquitous is the shelving unit. Many modern shelving designs are sold as flat packs for home assembly, and form part of a modular system that can be expanded as your storage needs increase. The untreated pine wood kits, originally intended for garages and garden sheds, are good value, as well as being sturdy and easy to assemble. Painted or finished with a coloured wood stain, they can also look extremely handsome.

Most modular units have the added advantage of adjustable shelving, making it possible to store and display anything from small books, personal items like framed photographs, a radio, computer disks or small tools and equipment to large boxes of documents, heavy equipment or oversize books. For the ultimate in flexibility choose from modern freestanding units on wheels: bookshelves, room dividers, filing cupboards and even whole home offices in a box. Wheel your office into position in the morning, then, at the end of the day, push it out of the way into a cupboard or another room.

types of shelving

Shelving is available in a wide range of design options, most of which fall into two main groups: systems with fixed supports and those that offer adjustability. If you are fairly certain of the items to be stored and do not expect them to change, fixed shelving will suit your needs. However, in many cases storage needs alter over time, and the option of adjustable shelves will help to accommodate them. The choice of shelving will depend not only on whether you expect your storage needs to change, but also on the weight of material the shelves will need to carry. It is worth noting that shelves held in place with only end supports are unlikely to be as good at weight bearing as shelves with back supports.

FIXED SHELVES

WALL-FIXED BRACKETS: Pairs of brackets are fixed directly to the wall, to support the shelves from behind. They come in various shapes and sizes, including the familiar triangular shape, or as short poles that provide support either by sitting under the shelf or by slotting in to the back of the shelf.

BATTEN SUPPORTS: Lengths of timber are fixed to the wall, to make a small ledge on which the shelf rests or is screwed into place. The ledge can support either end of the shelf and, for extra support, can be run along the back of the shelf, too. Strong, but not always aesthetically pleasing.

SCREW OR DOWEL FIXING: Shelves are secured using wooden dowels or screws driven horizontally through the upright support into the shelf end.

ADJUSTABLE SHELVES

RAILS AND BRACKETS: Slotted metal rails are fixed to the wall behind the shelf. Triangular brackets are hooked into the slots and the shelf sits on top. Tough, but not that attractive.

STRIPS AND CLIPS: Metal strips with slots are fixed to the wall, then small clips are fitted into the slots to hold the shelf ends. A useful method of fixing shorter shelves at either end.

HOLES AND POLES: Pairs of holes are drilled at 5–10cm (2–4in) intervals into an upright piece of wood. A small wooden or brass dowel is pushed into each, and protrudes a small amount to take the weight of the shelf. Useful for supporting shelves at either end.

organizing storage

The best organization ensures that items in frequent use are closest to you. Think of yourself as the hub of a series of concentric circles. As they radiate out from the centre, they represent storage areas for items in varying degrees of use; that is, the less often something is used, the further away it can be stored. The best place for most material in frequent use is the desk and a nearby area of shelves fixed between waist and shoulder height. Items will be readily accessible, so you will not have to stretch or bend down too often.

The desktop should be home to most things needed throughout the day. These will be within arm's reach while you are seated. After that, the storage plan depends on the size and shape of your office space. Items used perhaps once a day can be stored on shelving or in units just a step away from the desk. Material needed only a couple of times a year should be stored furthest away.

Obviously, the size and shape of items are important factors in how they are stored. For the best ergonomic design, small, light items should be stored at the top of units, and heavier items placed lower down. There are exceptions: for example, heavy files in regular use are best stored at mid-height and close to the worktop, so that they can be lifted easily or slid off the shelf and on to the worktop. Make sure that full, bulky files and boxes are properly sealed so that they remain closed when lifted from the shelf.

A management routine to keep the amount of storage in the office under control is essential. Depending on the work undertaken, some offices can function well with an annual spring-clean, while others may require a monthly check-up. Take a look at files and shelves, and weed out any items that are no longer in regular use. If they are still needed, but only occasionally, store them somewhere else altogether, such as in a cellar, attic or garage. When items become redundant, be sure to throw them away, recycling where possible (see pages 54–5).

OPPOSITE *This wardrobe-style arrangement is an inexpensive and effective way of screening office paraphernalia in a shared-use space such as a bedroom.*

RIGHT *There is hardly a scrap of wasted space here, with shelves climbing up and over the door to the ceiling. Little-used books are reached by a ladder, which is hooked over a metal rail fixed to the upper shelves. Stabilizers hold the ladder firmly in place on the floor.*

clever ideas

No matter how good the storage design, there is always room for another clever idea. The following might inspire and help with awkward items.

A WALL-FIXED pigeonhole unit is ideal for small items, such as a stapler, pencil sharpener, computer disks and spare ink cartridges.

A RANGE of full-height cupboards with flush-fit or sliding doors along a hallway can provide lots of additional storage space.

BUILT-IN SHELVING that covers every inch of the wall, including up and over the door, will provide much more generous storage space than freestanding shelving units.

A ROOM DIVIDER is a useful device for screening off an office in a dual-use room, and it provides additional storage capacity.

WHERE AN OFFICE is in a living area, consider buying storage units on wheels, so you can move them out of the way easily after work.

LOOK AROUND THE HOME for useful pockets of storage space: under the stairs, the bottom of a coat cupboard, inside a window seat, a dry basement, garden shed or garage.

WHERE THE OFFICE is integrated into the home, traditional items of furniture such as dressers and wardrobes can be transformed to provide huge amounts of office storage space.

lighting

The primary function of good office

lighting is to create a comfortable

and stimulating workspace

lighting overview

Natural light is hard to beat for its even quality and ease on the eye. The best artificial lighting schemes imitate natural lightfall, achieved by an even spread of ambient lighting with desk lamps for work needing close concentration. Angle computer screens at 90 degrees to the window to avoid direct sun glare.

In any office, it must be possible to see well, without eye strain and without glare, and to be able to work unhindered to the best of your ability. We are all extremely light sensitive and respond instinctively to the light around us.

Bright Mediterranean sunlight possesses a feel-good factor, which is invigorating and uplifting; it has quite the opposite effect of natural light over a northern European city on an overcast and wet winter's day, when our instinct is to retreat and cocoon ourselves. Because we react well to good, clear natural light, when there is not enough of it to work by, we need to supplement it with artificial light. The optimum levels for working are midway between the extremes of bright Mediterranean light and the dull grey light of winter. Ideally, the light should illuminate a space evenly without glare and without too many dark shadows.

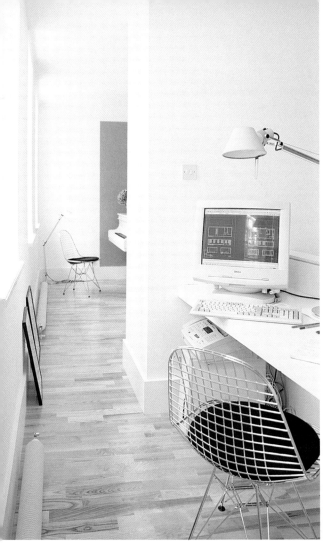

The starting point of any home-office lighting design scheme is to assess the natural light already available in the room. Broadly speaking, in the northern hemisphere, north- and north-east facing rooms receive a cooler, more even light than south- and south-west-facing rooms. The north-facing studio has always been favoured by artists because the light it receives is more constant and has fewer variations than the light pouring in from the south. South-facing rooms tend to suffer from too much strong sunlight, which brings with it heat. Rooms facing due east will get the morning sun and the evening setting sun will flood in from the west.

You will always need to supplement natural light with artificial lighting on dull days, dark winter mornings and afternoons, and for those occasions when you have to work late. Although you probably already have artificial lighting in your homeworking area, it is likely to need more support. Because our bodies are sensitive to light, it is necessary to manipulate our physical and emotional responses when we are working. For example, a living room lighting scheme that uses a central pendant lamp and two table lamps will be perfectly comfortable and suitable for relaxation and entertaining, but no good at all for working in. Our bodies are tuned instinctively to the daily cycle of the sun and know that low lighting levels come in the evening when it is time to rest and sleep. In order to work efficiently, we need more stimulation and increased light levels that imitate natural daylight. For concentrating on detailed and complex tasks we need more light still, and the older we get the more light we need to see accurately. It is worth noting, too, that poor office lighting does more than just affect our emotions and performance: it can have an adverse physical effect, causing eyestrain, which, in turn, can cause tension in the neck and shoulder muscles, as well as provoke headaches.

ABOVE RIGHT *Natural light enters this roof space through a long horizontal window, which is fitted with a pull-down blind to diffuse the brightest light. A ceiling track is used to bounce artificial light off the walls and a desk lamp provides important task lighting for close-up work such as reading and drawing.*

ABOVE LEFT *This small office space built into a corridor between rooms is well illuminated with sunlight from windows and a desk lamp that sheds extra light on the work area. White walls reflect the light and give the space an open feel.*

lighting quality

Once you have decided where to locate your home office and you start to build up a picture of how it is to be furnished and decorated, you can then introduce lighting to the mix.

The first thing to do is assess the natural light in the work space: make a note of how it changes through the day, where the brightest light falls and where any shadows are cast. A generous helping of natural light is more than just easier on the eye than artificial sources; it also saves money on fuel bills. So, if you have the opportunity, you might consider enlarging windows or adding rooflights to bring in more natural light. At this point decide whether you want curtains or blinds at the windows, or nothing

at all: curtains will tend to block the light following into the room, while cloth roller blinds and Venetian blinds will provide a soft filter for harsh light. If you suffer from glare on your computer screen, whether from natural or artifical light, find ways of diffusing the light, perhaps with a cotton blind or muslin net, or reposition the screen away from the direct source.

Take care in choosing your source of light, too. The regular household bulb is tungsten light that is slightly soft and yellow. For crisper, bluer light opt for tungsten halogen lamps. Or try a mixture of the two: tungsten for general lighting and halogen for highlighting and task lamps.

The other major consideration is the décor. Rooms painted in paler tones will, of course, reflect more light than those in darker colours, but there are other considerations besides wall and ceiling colour. For example, texture plays an important role in manipulating light: matt and textured surfaces absorb more light than glossy, smooth ones.

types of artificial lighting

When choosing your lighting, it is important to differentiate between the various light sources available for the home office and to appreciate their individual properties.

TUNGSTEN: These are the bulbs we are most familiar with. They have changed little in the century since they were invented, and are simply a glass dome containing a filament that glows when charged with electricity. They are available in clear, pearl or coloured glass, and in their clear state offer a yellowish light. The bulbs are now produced in a huge range of shapes and sizes; they tend to be widely available and very inexpensive. They are, however, far from energy efficient and have a relatively short life, lasting around 1,000 hours.

TUNGSTEN HALOGEN: Relatively new on the market, tungsten halogen produces a nice sharp, white light by using direct mains power. The quality of light has found lots of admirers, and the small bulbs and modern light fittings are becoming more widely available. The lifespan is at least double that of a regular tungsten bulb, but they are more expensive.

LOW-VOLTAGE TUNGSTEN HALOGEN: A real sparkling success, these small, bright lights are snapped up by anyone wanting to add fresh, crystalline light to their home and office. The drawbacks are that the bulbs are very expensive and are rarely sold in local hardware stores. Also, the fittings include hefty transformers to convert the mains supply for their use, which can make an annoying hum if used with dimmer switches. However, they have a really long life, up to 3,500 hours, are very energy efficient, and there is nothing like low-voltage halogen spotlights to add drama and interest to a room.

FLUORESCENT: These used to be everyone's idea of nightmare lighting – long flickering strips producing a nasty sickly light – but in recent years the technology has improved enormously to make lights that are kinder on the eye. Also available are compact fluorescents, which resemble large lightbulbs and are incredibly energy efficient. Because fluorescent lights contain a cocktail of chemicals, most manufacturers advise that they are disposed of carefully.

OPPOSITE LEFT *These large windows allow in so much natural sunlight that additional artificial lighting is needed only on very gloomy days. The domestic-looking desk lamps are stylish and effective.*

OPPOSITE RIGHT *A ceiling-mounted track with low-voltage halogen lamps adds sparkle to the lighting system, which runs from the office into the adjoining living area.*

light fittings

ABOVE *The industrial style of this monochrome home office, with metallic desk and chair, is picked up in the light fittings with stainless steel desk lamps.*

In recent years there has been an explosion in the number and variety of light fittings on the market; at last, high-street stores are stocking interesting fittings once available only through trade suppliers.

The traditional table lamp has been joined by thousands of innovative designs, from flamboyant, reproduction Venetian glass chandeliers to reissued lava lamps from the 1970s. Also new to the mix is an increasingly broad choice of sturdy industrial light fittings, including big, factory-style, stainless steel pendant shades, bulkhead lights, floodlights and high-powered, waterproof, outdoor light fittings.

RIGHT *A dramatic quartet of large, single lamps is suspended from the ceiling over the central table in this spacious and minimal home office. The curtainless windows let in as much natural light as possible, and the pale tones of the room add to the light and open feel.*

fittings for effects

UPLIGHTING: As the name suggests, an uplighter throws light upwards to reflect off the walls and ceiling to give a soft indirect light. This effect can be achieved through wall-mounted lights or freestanding units, such as standard lamps. For both types of fitting, the majority of light is prevented from falling downwards as the light bulb is set in an opaque holder.

DOWNLIGHTING: This can be used for adding a wash of illumination or as a directional beam through ceiling-recessed and pendant light fittings. Some of the most beautiful downlighting effects are achieved with low-voltage halogen lamps; tracks of lights throw washes of light down walls, while single lamps create dramatic pools of light on floors or at

whatever object they are pointed. Halogen lamps are available in a variety of voltages, and in various designs to cast different beam widths.

SPOTLIGHTING: Spotlights provide the means to highlight an area or object with a narrow and often intense beam of light. Different effects will be achieved depending on the direction of the light. Whether it is from above, below or the side, it is an extremely effective way of drawing attention to a particular feature.

TASK LIGHTING: This term refers to desk lamps, such as the classic Anglepoise, which sit on the worktop and provide intense, directed light over the work area.

ABOVE *Simplicity is often the key to a successful lighting scheme. An articulated lamp with a heavy base provides the necessary additional light to illuminate this desk.*

RIGHT *In this exciting clash of styles, an ancient timbered house is adapted for modern usage with a high-tech office scheme and chunky industrial lamps clamped to metal supports on wheels.*

Domestic-style table and standard lamps and hanging pendants will probably always look best in rooms decorated and furnished in a traditional way. However, modern fittings are likely to work equally well in traditional and contemporary settings. For something unusual, consider a lighting system on a track, fixed to the ceiling in straight lines or curves, clusters of pendant lamps hanging over a central work table, lights inset into the floor, or a bold clash of fitting styles, for example, an ornate candelabra or chandelier in the centre of the room supported by lots of twinkling, low-voltage halogen spotlights to highlight details.

RIGHT In this workspace, which is clearly used only occasionally, the domestic-style table lamp is totally in keeping with the rest of the interior décor while, at the same time, providing essential task lighting.

ten tips when choosing lighting

TO BOOST the natural lightfall, consider enlarging windows or swapping curtains for blinds.

DECIDE which sort of light source you prefer: tungsten, tungsten halogen, low-voltage halogen or fluorescent.

CHECK local availability for replacement bulbs if you select halogens.

IF YOU PLAN to have an entire new lighting system with different sorts of lights, check with a qualified electrician whether your existing domestic system will be able to cope with the load.

MAKE SURE the fittings will complement and enhance the office décor.

CONSIDER industrial lighting: it is strong and durable and often exciting in style.

TAKE A LOOK at lighting options offered by office furniture suppliers; some of the recent designs are stunning to look at as well as effective.

DECIDE whether dimmer-operated fittings will be beneficial.

DON'T CHOOSE fittings solely by their appearance; always switch them on to see how the light falls.

FIND OUT the degree of flexibility that the fitting allows; do you need directional light, perhaps a desk lamp with a movable arm?

designing with light

By this stage you will have a clear idea of the natural light available in your home office and the different types of artificial lighting on the market. The next step is to piece together an overall scheme or map.

The aim is to build up a comfortable level of all-round, ambient light and then provide brighter pools of light for areas of intense work, and perhaps spotlighting for artworks or architectural detailing. Approach it as if you were painting the room with light, by starting with an overall wash of light and then adding in extra interest with highlights.

With ambient lighting, it is almost always the case that you will need more light sources than you first think, and it is usually better to have four lamps of medium brightness than just a couple that are intensely bright. Bright lights will cause glare, hard shadows and may lead to eyestrain and headaches. Being able to control the brightness with a dimmer switch can be a real bonus.

The room where you establish your home office is likely to already have a pendant light, but you will still need back-up lighting, since the light provided by pendant lights is ugly and unflattering, and casts shadows in the corners of the room. So, build on this central source and, depending on the size of the room, add lighting at table- or desk-height in the form of table lamps. Translucent paper or fabric shades will soften the lightfall.

I would also recommend lighting three-quarters of the way up the wall with a standard lamp or wall lights. Providing a wash of light on walls makes a room feel larger and adds a pleasing diffuse and reflected light. Finally, select at least one good task light; this is most likely to be a desk lamp. Fixed lamps will not allow you to focus the light where it is most needed, so I would suggest an articulated lamp with a heavy base. The base anchors the light source and allows it to be moved to exactly the right position. If a lot of your work is computer-based, look for a lamp that can be angled directly over the keyboard without casting shadows as you work. An articulated lamp will also allow you to move it out of the way when not required. Other varieties of task lamp can be wall mounted: their fittings are mounted on arms which can be swung into and out of position over the worksurface.

In addition to this basic setup, there are endless possibilities for unusual and eyecatching sources of light. Spotlights are perfect for highlighting and ading drama. For something a little more unusual, why not consider floor-mounted lamps? The range has expanded enormously in recent years. I have seen 1m- (3ft-) high paper pyramids, unusual 2m- (6ft-) high basket weave towers, and even beautiful plastic moulded lamps in the shape of oversize pebbles. You can also experiment with neon and fluorescent lighting: setting fluorescent strips above a unit of book shelves can produce a distinctive ceiling wash, while industrial-style bulkhead lamps and wall washers add interest. At the small-scale end of lighting design, tiny spot lamps can be built into the underside of shelves, to cast a twinkling light on the surface below.

OPPOSITE *This dramatic lighting scheme in an attic home office certainly means business and lifts the tempo. Low-voltage halogen spotlights twinkle while heavy-duty industrial uplighters wash ceilings and walls with a soft, diffused light, to open up the space.*

ABOVE *A corner desk in a pale-painted room benefits from natural sunlight streaming in through the window and ambient light from the central pendant. An articulated desk lamp provides the necessary task lighting. The cleverly placed mirror reflects sunlight into the corner of the room.*

planning your space

Once you have decided what elements

you want your home office to contain,

it is time to map them into the space

planning overview

Whether you are creating your home office from scratch or upgrading an existing one, a set of plans is important in imposing some discipline and order on your thoughts. The aim is to make the best use of the available space, to create a workstation that functions efficiently, and to ensure that your office is an environment that is a pleasure to be in. For example, if you are fortunate enough to have a gorgeous view overlooking your garden and you have the space and means to place your desk near a window, don't hesitate to do so.

The first step to take when planning is to make a list of all the items that you want included in the office, right down to the mousemat and pencil pot. Next, make a measured sketch or drawing of the space into which the office has to fit.

Although measuring sounds such a simple task, if it is done badly or incompletely, it can wreak havoc. My advice would be to measure just about everything: the width and height of the walls, doors and windows, measuring to the outside of the frames and their distance from the floor and ceiling,

RIGHT *This orderly example of space planning puts items in regular use close to the desktop and less frequently used reference material on a shelf around the corner.*

OPPOSITE *A made-to-measure, curved desk fits the bay window perfectly, giving the space a pleasing flow. The computer is tucked away in the corner below shelves, and the largest portion of desktop is lit by natural sunlight from the window. Drawer units fit under the desk. It is an inviting and inspiring space.*

LEFT *This streamlined office, which looks and feels thoughtfully planned, doubles as a guest bedroom. Storage is generous and discreet, so the desktop can easily be cleared when there are visitors. When the room functions as an office, the sofabed is used for reading reports.*

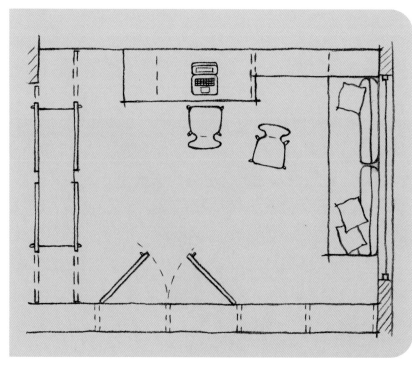

so that you know precisely how much space they take up. It is also a good idea to mark in existing electrical sockets, light switches, fittings, radiators, heating pipes, telephone sockets and the location (if known) of any underfloor services.

Architectural drawings come in two basic types: the three-dimensional and the two-dimensional. The former are much more difficult for the unskilled to draw, but their advantage is that they offer the best outline visualization of the space. Two-dimensional drawings come in three basic types: the bird's-eye view plan (looking at the floor layout from above, as though the room has been sliced through horizontally), the section (looking sideways at a slice of the inside of the building) and the elevation (looking at a view of the exterior). To get a good idea about how your home office design might work in practice, you will probably need only bird's-eye view plans to start with.

Once you have drawn the basic layout of the room, keep it as a master and photocopy it a few times; copies will allow you to experiment with different design options. Try an assortment of layout sketches and rough plans to check which ideas work the best. If you want to move from paper to the screen, there are plenty of software programs for designing room layouts on the market. As well as being great fun to play around with, you will be able to print out the results.

LEFT *This floor-to-ceiling room divider, which separates the home office from the living area, is also an ingenious piece of storage. When the doors are slid across the openings, shutting off the room beyond and ensuring privacy, bookshelves are revealed.*

OPPOSITE FAR LEFT, TOP AND ABOVE *These architectural drawings – bird's-eye view, three-dimensional and section – are all plans of the home office featured on page 90. The three-dimensional plan is the easiest to read but the most difficult to draw.*

step-by-step design

Planning takes as its starting point the availability of space, time and budget. A limited budget and small office area will leave little room for manoeuvre, but you should be able to do clever things with storage, to use every scrap of space.

In an ideal world the home office design begins with you. Ask yourself where you want to sit: most people prefer not to have their back to a door and will always like a view outside, if there is one to be had. Don't just think about arranging furniture around the walls; perhaps a desk in the centre of a room could work, or maybe it could be set at right angles to the wall. Consider the position of electrical sockets. It is relatively inexpensive to add or move them to fit in with your design, and always plan in at least a couple of spares, as you are bound to need more than you think. With the desk and chair in place, make sure your computer screen is not reflecting direct glare from the sun. Finally, fit your storage system around the desk, remembering that items in regular use should be closer to the hub.

In a dual-use room, assess how the two uses will mesh together. If the office doubles as a guest bedroom, you can let the office function rule until the next guest arrives, in which case it is helpful to be able to tidy away as much of the everyday clutter as quickly as possible. When the office is shared with a heavily-used area such as a living or dining room, you will need discipline and storage to keep stray business-related material under control. A file unit on wheels would probably be a sound investment in such a situation. Sometimes referred to as a 'puppy' or 'donkey', the unit can be pulled out of the way after work hours.

better by design

Space planning is a difficult blend of art and science. Keep in mind the practicalities of accommodating all your work-related material, at the same time taking care to ensure the work environment is inspiring, exciting as well as uplifting.

START WITH YOU, your desk and your chair. Take advantage of any available natural light, and treat yourself to a view if possible.

TRY SEVERAL different configurations, even experimenting with the desk in the middle of the room, just to see how it works.

MAKE SURE you have enough power sockets; be generous in your calculations.

PLAN YOUR STORAGE: frequently-used items should be closest to the desk.

IN DUAL-USE ROOMS, build-in cupboards or storage units to facilitate packing away work material when the room is not in use as an office.

IN A SINGLE-USE OFFICE, and with space permitting, make room for a soft area for taking breaks or holding meetings.

IF THERE IS ADDITIONAL free space, add a lavatory or a tea- and coffee-making area.

DEVISE your lighting plan.

LEFT *This home office is designed to reflect the contemporary style of the rest of the apartment. The white paintwork and pale grey flooring is continued throughout the living and working space.*

BELOW *An accomplished piece of space planning, this home office works as an L-shape, following the line of the circulation route at the side of the living space. There are cupboards below desktop height and open shelving above. The desk sits at the far end under the arched window, to make the most of the natural light.*

Where you have the chance of dedicating a room solely to business use and there is space left over, think about making a soft area with a sofa or a couple of armchairs, either for meetings or for taking a break, reading a paper, going through reports, or even having a nap. You could also add a small table for meetings. Where there is a real luxury of space, consider an extra lavatory so that visitors do not have to walk through the rest of the house, or perhaps a tea- and coffee-making area?

With a clear design emerging, map in your lighting needs, making sure you blend general room lighting with desk-based task lighting, and perhaps additional spotlights lights for dramatic effect.

working in style

Among the most appealing aspects of

working at home is having ultimate

control over how your space looks

style overview

With rare exceptions, the corporate office interior is designed as a neutral backdrop to the day-to-day business of work. It offends no one, but at the same time it delights no one. However, your home office can be created exactly as you wish. If you want to work in a stripped-bare white box or have clutter up to the ceiling, it is your choice.

By this stage of the design process, you will know exactly what equipment and furniture you want to have in the office and how it will all be organized within the space. So, the final flourish is the style in which that is accomplished.

Now you have the opportunity to express your personality and make a space that reflects who you are and what you do. If you have meetings with clients at your office, take time to think about the impression you want to give them and how that can be matched with the office of your dreams. If you have an entire room to devote to your office, you may feel inspired to create a different scheme from one that you would choose for a dual-use space. But if your office is shared with another room, decide whether it is the office or the other room that should take style precedence.

Finally, always keep your budget in mind. In my experience, it is wise to invest in good quality basics, such as flooring, cupboards, shelves, curtains and blinds, and go for the less expensive decorating option: a backdrop of painted walls will give you the flexibility to change the colour scheme quickly and easily, and it is certainly more cost-effective than replacing the furnishings.

LEFT *A truly distinctive and highly personalized space, with an amazing collection of colourful glassware and an intriguing sculptural chair.*

OPPOSITE *An exploration of designer decay with the rough-edged plasterwork around the doorway and fireplace offset by the highly glossy floor and neat paintwork on the walls. The home office is a small, contained unit fitted into the corner of the dining area.*

which style?

Before settling on a specific style of décor for your home office, think first about the way in which you work and the mood you wish to create. The idea is to take an objective stance and imagine seeing the space through the eyes of an interior designer.

Begin by analysing the emotional content of the space. What should your ideal office feel like? Identify the types of schemes that you find inspiring, that make you feel good, lift the spirits and help concentration. For some, this will mean a simple, minimally finished room, while others will prefer a more domestic setting, surrounded by familiar items such as photographs and pictures.

Think about how and where you work best. Ask yourself whether you want the space to reflect your personality, and whether that will fit in with how you want to be perceived by visiting clients. If your instinct is to use bold colours and flamboyant furnishings, are you sure that your clients will feel comfortable with such a look? A lot does depend on the type of work you do, but consider whether you should tone down your ideas or camp them up.

As for the furniture: should it be in a corporate office style or domestic-looking, or be something a little more unusual? And the furnishings: simple roller blinds or softer curtains? Collect brochures, paint charts, wallpaper, carpet and fabric samples; cut out pictures from magazines. If you have a pinboard, make a mood collage with them.

This wonderful industrial montage is the home office version of the kitchen island: an all-in-one unit comprising conference table and worktop, computer workstation, drawing table, flip-up counter, storage and even a fridge.

dual-use or dedicated office?

From the first trawl of images and ideas, you will need to edit and make changes as you gradually piece together the design jigsaw. The final look of your home office depends to a great extent on its location within the home.

The single-use space offers the potential for a design scheme that can be quite different in tone and style from the rest of the home. If you wish, you can create a space with a serious business feel, making a clear distinction between home and office life. If you are concerned that these two lives may blur into one, design is an effective way of marking the boundaries. With such a scheme it is quite clear not only to you but also to everyone else when you are working and when you are not; at the end of the day, the door is closed and your leisure time and family life begin. The single-use space also provides the opportunity for a boldly themed environment. If you have always fantasized about working in a log cabin, or even a 1950s diner, or have hankered after a wild colour scheme, now is the chance to make those dreams a reality.

In a dual-use space the decorating approach is likely to be different. When workspace is allocated in a living room or bedroom, or even a kitchen, you have two choices. Either the scheme has to be fairly

well mannered so that it works with the existing furnishing style and colour scheme, or it sets the style for a completely new look in the whole room.

Although working at home is rapidly becoming a fact of life for many, few people want to live in a state of permanent muddle with papers and files a constant reminder of work. But provided that your storage is well organized and the furniture looks good, the home office can co-exist happily with any other aspect of your home life. If you plan to make a living working at home, the least you can do is make the experience enjoyable by creating the most comfortable and inspiring environment possible.

ABOVE *With a home office as stylish as this, who needs to worry about disguise? The chunky, oversized furniture sits comfortably in a large, understated living room.*

OPPOSITE LEFT *As the home office becomes an increasingly common part of everyday life, the latest computers are designed to fit in perfectly with modern domestic settings.*

OPPOSITE RIGHT *It seems appropriate for a home office to be accommodated in a building converted from industrial use. The abundant light let in by the enormous windows makes this a desirable living and working space.*

which colours?

Colour affects us emotionally and can hit right at the subconscious, to change our moods and impair or enhance performance. It is even believed to affect our health, either positively or adversely.

The effective handling of colour in interiors is a skill. When done well, the results can be astounding, making a room a real pleasure to be in. But get it wrong and the space will feel uncomfortable and uninviting, and you cannot wait to turn round and leave. There are no golden rules about how to use colour, but here I include guidelines for creating moods to match your style of office. Most paint manufacturers sell sample pots, so you can always experiment with a range of different colours before setting to work on an entire room.

There are many examples of the power of colour in influencing behaviour. Some prisons have certain cells painted a soft pink, to calm down aggressive or troubled inmates; in factories, harsh lime greens are occasionally used in lavatories, to

A tranquil backdrop helps to keep the nerves steady and the mind focused during a busy working day. In this largely monochrome office, the single pale colour unifies the space and delivers a sense of calm.

deter workers from lingering, and restaurants are frequently painted red, to raise blood pressure and stimulate the tastebuds. I know of an advertising agency that has colour-coded its meeting rooms according to the psychological effect that it wants to promote: the room for long, thoughtful meetings is painted blue, a colour usually associated with creativity. For medium-length meetings that require quite serious concentration, a sage green is used, to provide a calm and focused atmosphere. The room for short meetings is painted an acrid acid yellow; decisions in this room are reached at top speed because no one wants to be surrounded by such an eye-searing colour for longer than they need.

Reminiscent of a traditional study, this richly painted workspace creates a more sombre mood. Although dark, saturated colours can be restful on the eye, some people may find them energy sapping.

Colours that are restful in a living room might be too laid-back for a home office, and if your office space is shared with another room, you may want to use colour to make the boundaries between home and work clearer. Of course, this depends on how you work: a laid-back atmosphere suits some people very well, but for others it is too much like home and concentrating on work becomes difficult. Think also of the different ways you use the space and respond to colours: your office may need to be brighter, sharper, more stimulating than the rest of the home, so in a dual-use office the working area could be picked out in a different colour by painting the wall behind the desk. Alternatively, you can keep the colours the same and define the space by boosting the levels of artificial lighting.

It might sound obvious but it is difficult to beat neutrals like stone, ivory and grey for a calm and contemplative, even sophisticated, interior. Lilac or pale creamy yellow are more unusual shades that will create a similar effect, and soft blues and green will be gentle on the eye. But that is not to say you should avoid strong colour; used well it can truly lift a space and add a welcome dash of interest.

Bold colours will always raise the tempo, but brighter, more forceful hues can become wearing. An entire office finished in turquoise or cerise pink, for example, will almost certainly feel oppressive after a while. But if your heart is set on adding a vibrant colour, paint one wall in the strong shade and the rest of the space white. For something more unusual, experiment with a broad horizontal band of colour around the walls, or paint the bottom half of the walls in a really bold shade, offset by a paler

tone above. Alternatively, a single wall of broad, vertical, multicoloured stripes or a chequerboard of colours could add just the zest you want.

When planning your colour scheme, take into account how the natural light falls: in the northern hemisphere, east-facing rooms receive the pale morning sunlight, south-facing rooms will be filled with stronger sunlight for most of the day, west-facing rooms will receive afternoon and evening sun, while north-facing rooms will receive no direct sunlight at all. In terms of colour, this means that cool blues, greens and neutral colours will look cooler, perhaps even chilly, in north- and east-facing rooms. Warmer reds, oranges and yellows will appear richer in west- and south-facing rooms.

TOP RIGHT *The sombre tones of this hallway office separate it visually from the adjoining kitchen and living space.*

OPPOSITE TOP RIGHT *The black rug contrasts powerfully with the lilac paintwork. It is an unusual combination but works particularly well combined with the metallic detailing in the chair and desk lamp.*

OPPOSITE BELOW *Red is known to be a stimulating colour – that is why it is used in so many restaurants. Here, it adds an accent, a dash of hot pepper, to spice up the pale blue colour scheme.*

the homeworkers

With advances in technology,

people from all professions are

choosing to work at home

garden pod

When Anna Ryder Richardson, the television interior designer, first saw her garden apartment, it was run down and in need of renovation. But, together with Rawden Rogerson from her design agency a² 2000, she transformed the once-unpromising space.

One of the most inspired features is Anna's home office: a light, glass-skinned pod that nudges out into the garden, drawing natural light into the apartment and providing valuable work space. Natural light is essential for Anna, who needs to be able to look at colour swatches and put together decorating schemes in good quality light.

The office leads out of the back of the house from what was once a small second bedroom. Anna has turned this into a cosy 'snug' or sitting room.

There had been a window in the back wall, but this soon became part of the new extension. Because the garden level was stepped up from the floor of the apartment, the first job was to dig out a quarter circle between the back wall of the house and side wall of the garden. The depth of this excavation work is just over one metre (3ft), and it has been lined and finished to form the curved inside wall of the office. Above this sits the distinctive glazed dome. For this, Anna made use of her contacts in the trade to locate a company specializing in the manufacture of skylights, domes and glazed panels for industrial buildings, such as factories.

The pod is constructed from a metal frame divided into four segments. Each segment contains the shaped glass that forms the roof and walls of the pod. Double glazing not only provides good insulation against heat loss in winter, but is also a shield against ultraviolet rays and prevents the interior from becoming too hot in summer. The pod works like a traditional conservatory, giving great garden views and offering protection from extremes of weather. A single window can be wound open manually to provide ventilation, and the pitch of the roof has been carefully calculated so that the rain washes off dust and leaves.

Inside the office, the walls are painted white for simplicity and to reflect the light. The garden walls have been painted white, too, for precisely the same reasons. Overall, the monochrome colour scheme makes for a tranquil and airy workspace.

Although the workspace is compact, Anna has managed to fit in a high, circular, café-style table with adjustable stools, which she uses for informal

Inevitably, the room plan for such a compact space is simple, but Anna has added interest to her office with a high-level, circular table that is ideal for informal meetings. Outside, the decking comes right up to the side of the pod, so that potted plants and flowers stand at eye level and can be enjoyed while Anna works.

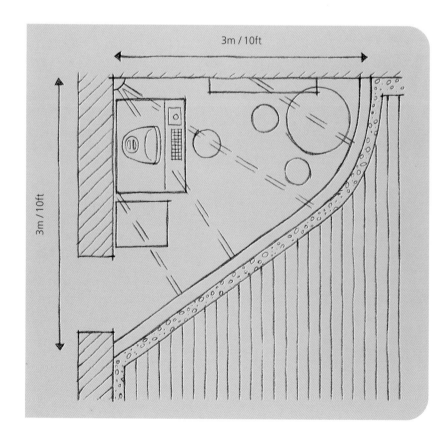

3m / 10ft

3m / 10ft

LEFT *Just like a traditional conservatory, the domed glass pod mushrooms out into the garden, helping to blur the boundary between inside and out. The pod is most striking at night when it glows in the corner of the garden.*

BELOW *The home office leads into the garden from a former small bedroom, now transformed into a cosy 'snug' or sitting room. There is no door separating the two areas, so during the day natural light is able to flow unimpeded into the heart of the living space.*

meetings. There is also ample storage space above and below the worktops that line the two right-angled walls, as well as a 1970s-style, freestanding, cylindrical bin for keeping fabric samples, swatch books, product manuals and colour cards out of sight. The walls have been kept as clear as possible, to reduce the visual clutter still further.

Lighting includes desk-mounted task lights, and at night the pod glows in the corner of the garden. Additional sparkle comes from garden spotlights.

garden pod

music room

Here is a contemporary interpretation of the grand library and music room that manages to be both a home office and a place for relaxation. Sophia is a book editor and through the course of her work has amassed a huge collection of books, which are now housed in this inviting and spacious office.

When Sophia and her family moved into their new home, it was in need of a makeover. For more than 30 years it had been used as a music school, and the rooms were lined with acoustic insulation material, which had become worn and shabby.

Today, the focus of the living space is a pair of interconnecting reception rooms. These are very grand spaces with lofty ceilings and beautifully proportioned tall windows. One of the rooms is now the family living area, complete with sofa and dining table; the other accommodates Sophia's office and a grand piano, which is a fitting continuation of the house's musical tradition.

Originally there were cupboards flanking the main doorway, but Sophia decided to remove their doors to reveal floor-to-ceiling shelving. There are even book shelves over the top of the door. To cope with Sophia's ever-expanding collection, a new four-section shelving unit has been built on the wall close to the large bay window. The main shelving area contains mostly novels, while the new section is for reference material, magazines and an eye-catching collection of white-spined biographies and letters. Also on the shelving are small sculptures, pictures

RIGHT *This generous-sized room is lined with shelving. The plan shows the desk on one side of the room and, facing it, the beautiful grand piano.*

OPPOSITE *The whole home is flooded with light. The original doors between the work and living space were removed some time in the past, but Sophia hopes to replace them so that her office can be cut off from the sounds of home life.*

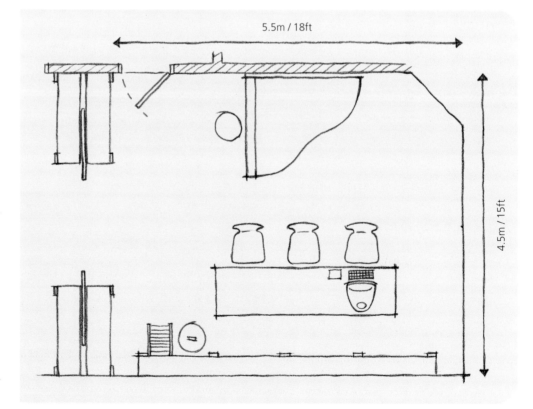

5.5m / 18ft

4.5m / 15ft

BELOW *Echoing the shelving that runs up and around the doorway, this large, wooden unit contains all the reference books and paperwork that Sophia uses regularly. The pale painted table is positioned close to the window to make the most of the natural light.*

OPPOSITE TOP LEFT *These neatly displayed pale volumes, all from the same publisher, are in marked contrast to the elegant black task lamp clamped to one of the shelves. When the lamp is switched on, the books act as a reflector, throwing diffused light back towards the desk.*

and storage boxes for small items and loose papers, such as bills, invoices and newspaper cuttings. The ladder was a gift from a neighbour; who had it as his means of escape in case of fire. When he replaced it with a more up-to-date model, he gave the old one to Sophia so that she could reach the highest shelves. She plans to add a horizontal metal pole around the top of the bookcases so that the ladder can be hooked on and held safely in place.

Standing in front of this shelving is a simple white-painted wooden table. It provides a worktop large enough for the computer, as well as space to spread out projects Sophia is working on, such as large page proofs for books. The table is also a favourite with the children, who love to join her in

RIGHT *Because the room is filled with natural light, Sophia is able to work for much of the day without additional artificial light. A shelving unit alongside the table holds the printer to free up work space.*

RIGHT *When Sophia needs a break from work, to gather her thoughts or simply to relax, she plays the grand piano.*

OPPOSITE ABOVE *Books cover the wall from floor to ceiling around the doorway, linking the home office to the living space. The shelves were originally closed cupboards but their doors have been removed, giving added interest to the room.*

OPPOSITE BELOW *This detail shows how the shelves run behind the fascia board – an idea borrowed from traditional cabinetwork. The raw, untreated timber adds texture and warmth to the scheme.*

the office to do their homework or to draw pictures. The printer sits on top of a small wooden shelving unit alongside the computer.

The room is well lit by natural sunlight but, of course, there are times when this needs boosting. A large and powerful uplighter is fitted to the library shelves around the door and there is a striking black lacquer modern light on the new shelving. This is cleverly positioned to throw light against the shelves of white-spined books, which in turn act as a reflector and bounce light back into the room, right by the worktable where it is most needed. On the worktable itself there are a couple of neat, stainless steel, low-voltage halogen task lights.

Taking pride of place in the centre of the room is the grand piano. When Sophia wants a break from work, she swaps her computer for the piano and practises her other keyboard skills.

law and orderliness

After working in cramped and busy law chambers, Daniel, a barrister, decided that to gain more space and peace he would bring his office home. A sunny spare bedroom with views over the garden was to become his new, tranquil work base.

To make the most of the available space, Daniel employed an architect. And because the new office had to accommodate a huge volume of paperwork, a design evolved to create a workroom lined from floor to ceiling and wall to wall with cupboards and shelving. No space is wasted – even the window is completely framed by the shelving, which swoops up and over the top. While the office obviously borrows elements such as its practicality from the traditional study, equally clear is its contemporary style. It is a bold piece of commissioning, producing a modern work space that is refreshingly removed from the stereotype of barristers' old-fashioned and cluttered chambers.

The built-in shelving and cupboard unit were inspired by the architect's own book shelving at home, but it has been reinterpreted here to suit Daniel's work needs. The cube module is based on the size of files he uses.

Birch-faced marine plywood, which measured a slender 18mm (¾in), was chosen for the bespoke units. Believed to have been invented by the ancient Egyptians, this sheet material is constructed in layers and is very strong. Ply is hailed as an environment-friendly product because it makes use of different grades of wood – less refined grades for the internal structure and a thin veneer of the best quality for

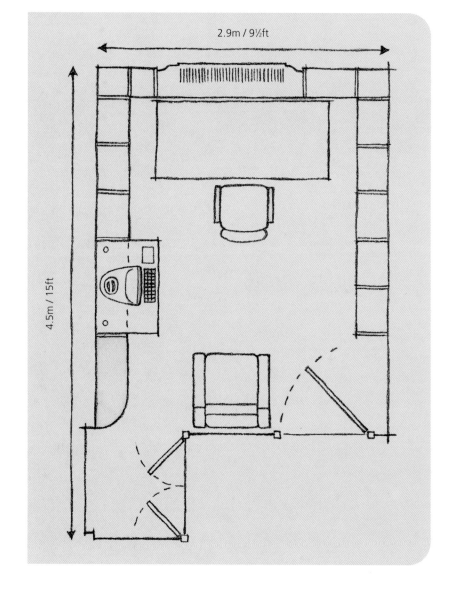

2.9m / 9½ft

4.5m / 15ft

LEFT *The desk takes pride of place by the window with a view of the garden. A separate worktop has been created to accommodate the computer, and the floor-to-ceiling shelving and filing drawers give generous storage space. The classic Le Corbusier leather chair is ideal for reading.*

OPPOSITE *This office is a reinvention of the traditional study. The use of light-coloured timber and pale carpet gives the room a warm glow, but the sleekly professional office chair, designed by Charles and Ray Eames, indicates that this is a business environment.*

ABOVE LEFT *Many workers in corporate offices dream of throwing open their window and letting in a soft breeze. Here is natural air-conditioning at its simplest. On bright sunny days the light is diffused by the cream-coloured blind. This office is calm and well ordered, yet personalized with pot plants and photographs, and is clearly a pleasure to work in.*

ABOVE RIGHT *The unusual desk was bought readymade from a high-street furniture retailer. The tapered legs support a pair of drawers and a couple of open shelves below. More by accident than design, the pale colour of the timber is a near-perfect match with the plywood used for the built-in shelving.*

the skin. For this home office, the design concept was to take a simple, inexpensive material and use it in a sophisticated way. Although often treated as a humble construction material – for lining floors and walls or boxing in pipework – here plywood sheeting is celebrated in its own right and gains dignity through superb craftsmanship.

The use of fine-grade ply creates an elegant effect, and the shelves and uprights look almost too delicate to support heavy books. If the shelves were wider, a thicker sheet would have been needed, but by creating a cubed system with short shelves, the interlocked units gain greater rigidity.

Set beneath the open shelving and wrapped around the lower part of the room are the filing drawers. Once again these have been tailor-made,

this time to accommodate barristers' files, which are larger than those generally used in offices. Satisfying details include the neat recessed handles cut away from the face of the drawer – no protruding knobs to disturb the sheer façade of the units or snag the clothing of anyone walking by.

The remaining storage area is found in a corner at the back of the room, where a walk-in cupboard provides space for archived files and documents. Although tucked away from the main office space, they are easily retrieved when needed.

The desk was found in a high-street furniture store, its colour a near-perfect match for the ply. Unusually, the design features a couple of drawers on each side and then two open shelves beneath. The shelves help to lighten the physical impact of the desk in its position against the window.

Daniel prefers to keep the view of his garden uninterrupted, and the desktop, which he uses primarily for taking notes and research, is kept as clear as possible. The computer is accommodated to one side of the room on a reinforced shelf made of three sheets of plywood, laminated together to make a rigid worktop strong enough to support the computer's weight. Above this workstation are the room's only adjustable shelves, which Daniel has found useful for storing small items.

Particularly appealing design details include the simple ply shelf over the less-than-attractive radiator, which sits below the window. To disguise the top of the radiator, the architect devised a plywood shelf with decorative but practical cut-out slots, to allow the heat to circulate.

Daniel's interest in classic modern furniture led him to buy the stunning leather and chrome office chair designed by the American duo Charles and Ray Eames. Behind this sits an armchair in the same materials – this time a Le Corbusier design – which provides comfortable seating when reading.

The shelving and drawer unit is a good example of modern craftsmanship. A cube design ensures that the shelves are fully supported and can take the weight of very heavy books without sagging. The computer desktop is made of three sheets of plywood to increase its strength.

attic seclusion

After he developed postviral fatigue (ME), media accountant Nick decided that he had to change his life completely. Until then, like millions of others, he had commuted daily to his city-centre office, but his illness became so debilitating he simply could not persevere. Gradually, as his health was restored, he was able to start doing some work from home. The convenience of this new-found work style became most apparent when the illness recurred and was at its worst. The prospect of going back to commuting became deeply unappealing.

At first, Nick considered renting an office close to home as he felt it was important to separate his work from his family life. However, after looking at several local office spaces, he discovered that renting would be an expensive commitment. His only other option was to investigate creating a home office.

Nick's house had a huge attic space which, although rather dark and dusty, had the potential for transformation into a useful working area. He calculated that the investment of converting the attic space would be less expensive than paying out monthly rent. And there was the added bonus of having an extra room in the house, which would enhance the property value.

Although he was convinced that the attic could be transformed into an office, Nick felt that an architect would be able to devise a scheme that was

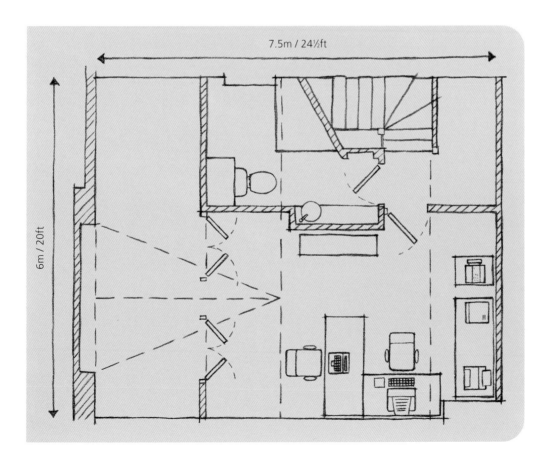

7.5m / 24½ft

6m / 20ft

LEFT *At first glance this home office may look like a fairly complex space. The plan shows the top of the stairs with one door leading to the shower and toilet, and another door leading to the office. The large triangle on the left indicates the pointed nook, which is used for reading and resting.*

OPPOSITE *Refreshingly unlike most accountants' offices, this space is crisp and modern. Remote storage in cupboards under the low parts of the sloping roof has allowed Nick to keep shelving to a minimum.*

RIGHT *Twin rooflights allow in plenty of natural light, even on fairly dull days, and at this height the office is open to the sky and not overshadowed by other buildings or trees. The desks are positioned so that it is possible to work in daylight most of the time, but a wall light and desk lamps help to supplement light levels when necessary.*

BELOW *The open-weave structure of this stainless steel shelving unit makes it ideal for boxes and files.*

considerably more imaginative and practical than anything he could sketch. The additional advantage was that the architect could also oversee the project, organizing and chasing after builders, which was a job Nick really did not relish.

The brief to the architect was to create a space that looked businesslike, and it was to stand quite apart in style from the family home. Because Nick knew that clients would need to visit occasionally for meetings, he felt it was necessary to create a professional setting. He resisted the temptation to

make the new home office into a dual-use space, perhaps as a guest bedroom, because he wanted to keep the focus solely for work use.

The architect has opened up the attic room to the apex of the roof to make generous headroom and has clawed back every single pocket of space. Built into the sloping roof, two large new windows draw in plenty of natural light.

One of Nick's favourite details is the conversion of a small corner nook, which is set apart from the main body of the room. This steeply pointed space, lit by a small window, is filled with cushions and makes a quiet bolt hole. It has a spiritual feel and is a space for reading, resting and contemplation. Nick uses it when his energy levels are low and when he wants a break from his busy schedule. Right at the head of the stairs, the architect has even found room to include a small toilet and shower room.

The finishes throughout the space are simple and hard edged. The off-white walls enhance the natural sunlight and provide a neutral backdrop free from distractions. The floor is finished in a rich, dark wood, chosen because it looks more like an office floor than a domestic one. Contemporary office furniture in black, chrome and stainless steel leaves no doubt at all that this is a serious professional office. In addition, the furniture sits well in the light and airy room, unlike heavy, dark wood furniture traditionally associated with accountancy offices, which would have closed in the space.

The two desks that form an L-shape provide plenty of worktop area, and there is even enough room for an assistant. The chairs have been carefully chosen for their ergonomic performance. As well as cupboard storage space, there is a white filing cabinet and a freestanding stainless steel shelving unit used to store box files, reports and magazines that are referred to everyday. Fitted with wheels, the unit can easily be moved around the office.

A tranquil retreat carved from the roofspace by the architect. It is separated from the main work area by a small step. Flanking the entrance and under the sloping roof are cupboards providing storage space for reports and documents not in regular use.

basement discovery

When Helen and Andrew moved house they seized the opportunity to turn a disused basement area into their office. Both of them worked at home and they needed a space that would accommodate Helen's work as a photographer and Andrew's as a live events producer.

The house was built in 1850. A section of the basement had originally been servants' quarters, but the space had remained unused since the Second World War. In fact, when the couple bought the house the low-ceilinged basement area was subject to a restriction called a closing order, which meant that it was unfit for human habitation.

This streamlined home office, which makes ingenious use of the available space, has been designed precisely to suit its two users. The rounded desktop is a generous working area and the curved shelf end provides clever storage for lever-arch files. Curves are ideal for offices – there are no sharp corners to bump into.

3.2m / 10½ft

4.1m / 13½ft

To completely transform the basement into a useful working office space, the only way to go was down. The floor was excavated and lowered to create vital additional ceiling height, and because the base of the room was below ground level, damp-proofing and other specialist measures were undertaken to make the space watertight.

In planning the office design, the demands of both occupants had to be taken into consideration. Helen needed by far the largest proportion of the space because she spends more time working at home. Andrew's requirements were more modest because he works away a great deal: a desk and filing space were sufficient. The design brief evolved with two key demands: generous storage space and, for aesthetic reasons, all cables and wiring had to be hidden. The couple designed and fitted out the office themselves.

Andrew knew from past experience that it was vital to build in as much storage space as possible at the outset. Even if it was not all necessary at first, he was certain that their collection of work-related material would expand considerably over the years. The result is that practically all the walls have been lined with shelves, drawers and cupboards. Even the chimneybreast has been hollowed out to make way for yet more shelving. The only real slice of unused space is around the base of the walls. Filing cabinets

OPPOSITE The basement is not blessed with generous amounts of natural light, but this pair of glass doors does allow light into the space. The walls facing the doors are painted white and kept free of pictures and pinboards so that they reflect light around the room.

and oversize publications. At the centre of this unit is a nest of small drawers, which was bought readymade and has been built in to the storage system. The drawer units make several appearances in the office and have proved particularly useful to Helen for stowing the many small items she uses every day, such as transparency sleeves, mounts, magnifying glasses and sticky labels.

One of the most ingenious details is the round-end shelving unit, which is specifically designed to accommodate large files. The curved end is a smart ergonomic feature; it cleverly averts any danger of bumping into a sharp desk corner, and provides a neat conclusion to the desktop. This rounded shape also makes perfect shelving for large lever-arch files which, because they are thickest at the spine, never sit properly on straight shelves.

Up to waist level, the walls are finished in wood panelling, which has been made to copy original panelling discovered in the basement. However, this finish performs more than just a decorative function. Behind it is threaded all the unsightly office cabling and wiring, and sections of the panelling can be removed to reveal large banks of electrical sockets. Once again, Andrew predicted accurately that, in time, additional sockets would be needed as more electrical equipment was bought for the office.

Of particular importance to both users was the colour scheme for the office. They wanted a tranquil backdrop to their work, something that was restful on the eye. A soft grey-green colour was chosen for the woodwork and, even after several years, the couple has not tired of it. In contrast, the walls and ceiling are painted white, to help boost the light

A useful inset shelving area, fitted with a drawer unit from a high-street store at its centre, has been created at the base of the stairs. Above the unit, a small cupboard provides additional storage.

and shelves stand approximately 15cm (6in) off the floor, to protect valuable paperwork just in case the basement should ever flood.

All the storage is in fixed, built-in units; even the filing cabinets sit inside a painted timber frame. And to accommodate the great variety of storage material, there is a mixture of open shelving and cupboards. At the base of the stairs, a purpose-built shelving unit has been made, to fit everything from CDs and video tapes to magazines, reports, files

LEFT *Neat drawers are useful for storing all the small items associated with Helen's work as a photographer: transparency sleeves, magnifying glasses, sticky labels, highlighter pens, plus the odd toy.*

ABOVE *Seen close-up, the curved-end shelf is an ingenious design for storing lever-arch files. These are difficult to accommodate on conventional straight shelves because they are almost always thickest at the spine.*

RIGHT *The tongue-and-groove wood panelling serves several functions in the office: it acts as a disguise for the part of the foundations that protrudes into the room and it hides all the sockets and cabling for the office equipment. It also looks extremely attractive.*

levels. Natural light flows down the stairs and cascades into the space through a pair of glazed doors. Where the sunlight is at its brightest, the walls are kept free of such obstructions as pinboards so that they act as reflectors. Ambient lighting is provided by ceiling-recessed spotlights, and the whole space is given a warm base with Mexican terracotta tiles, which were chosen because they are hardwearing and easy to clean.

basement discovery

in the frame

Nathalie and her partner Robert had been running their photographic agency from rather cramped, city-centre quarters, so when the couple decided to move to the outskirts of town, it made sense to look for a property large enough to accommodate the business, too. Their search led them to a beautiful 1930s building that now houses the agency on the ground floor with their home above.

The ground floor had been divided into small rooms, and so the first move in the refurbishment plans was to open up the area and make a single work space. Not surprisingly for people working in the photographic industry, the organization of the space was informed by light. The two tailor-made desks were placed against one wall to make the most of the sunlight, which is diffused by aluminium Venetian blinds when it becomes too harsh and glaring. Natural light was considered slightly less important for meetings and conferences, so the main table was placed in the centre of the room. A kitchen and an informal waiting area, complete with upholstered sofa and armchair, are positioned along the wall opposite the desks.

To support the generous natural light in the space, there is a well-considered artificial lighting scheme. Task lights sit on both desktops and, to illuminate the large purple-coloured cupboard that stands between them, there is a ceiling-mounted track with two high-voltage spotlights positioned to shine into the cupboard when the doors are slid

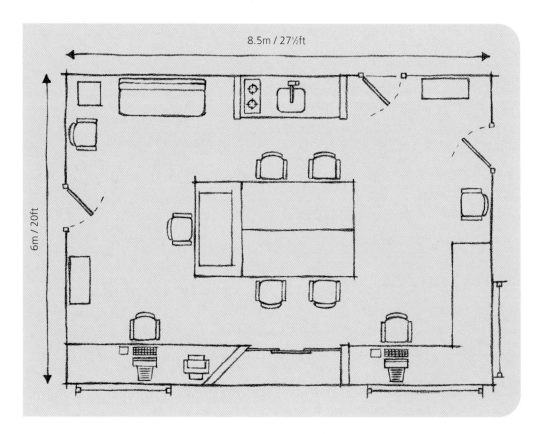

This home office has two large desks close to the windows, to make the most of the natural light. There is an upholstered waiting area for guests and a small kitchen, which is in constant use for making drinks and working lunches. The meeting and lunch table takes central position.

open. Suspended over the central table are two large industrial-style ceiling lamps and at one end of the table there is a large inset lightbox, which provides an illuminated surface on which to view transparencies. The kitchen area is lit with tiny low-voltage halogen lamps set into the underside of the cupboards and shelves. At the far end of the room there are two large industrial halogen lamps fitted three-quarters of the way up the walls. These act as

uplighters pointed at the ceiling and produce a wash of light. Robert was particularly pleased to have found these lamps in a grey metallized finish; they are usually sold in black and he specifically wanted grey. It took a while to source them, but he and Nathalie are delighted with the results.

Storage was also a major consideration in the planning of the room. The agency had previously been squeezed into tiny quarters, so the new space

The 1930s building provides lots of natural light with this entire corner given over to windows. The L-shaped workstation has a generous desktop and there is plenty of room for storage cabinets underneath.

an enormous capacity for a range of items including files, magazines and stationery. In addition, it houses all the electrical sockets and cabling supplies to the computers, printers, fax machine and telephones. When it comes to the company's vast archive of photographic imagery and magazines, this material is accommodated in well-ordered files in a separate small room leading from the main office.

Because the office is a social place and receives a number of visitors – there are regular meetings with photographers and magazine picture editors, for example – the kitchen has become an extremely important element in the overall design. It is not

BELOW Bold colours are used with confidence and the whole space is carefully lit with a mixture of light fittings. This is one of the industrial halogen lamps with a grey metallized finish that proved so difficult to track down – the design is commonly produced in black.

A soft upholstered waiting area is also used for informal meetings. Longer discussions are held at the conference table, where working lunches, prepared in the adjacent small kitchen, are also served.

provided an opportunity to create a storage system that would really help the smooth running of the business. A number of small filing units sit below the workcounters to store items that are in regular daily use, but most of the office-related storage is contained in the large purple-coloured, floor-to-ceiling cupboard built in between the two desk areas. This neat cupboard with its sliding doors has only used for making drinks, but also for preparing working lunches and, when there are deadlines to be met, late suppers as well. The units are regular kitchen cupboards. Inset into the top there is an industrial-style stainless steel sink and to its left a two-ring burner designed for use in professional kitchens. A shelf and cupboards for storing crockery and a small but well-stocked larder are within arm's reach above the sink.

Perhaps one of the most surprising aspects of this working space is the bold use of colour and lack of pictures on the walls. Nathalie had very firm ideas about the colour scheme, which has been greatly influenced by the Mexican architect Luis Barragan. His love of strong, saturated colours is picked up in the office: along with the purple-coloured cupboard, there is a solid purple wall and great slabs of pink, red and yellow.

Because their work involves looking at minutely detailed images, Nathalie and Robert wanted to avoid yet more imagery on the wall. So, they chose colours in large panels, to provide welcome visual respite from the complexity of the transparencies.

BELOW LEFT Where a wall once divided the space there is now a large purple-coloured cupboard for storing magazines, files and much of the office-related material.

BELOW Nathalie makes the most of natural light by placing her desk close to the window. Meetings with photographers and clients are held at the central conference table, which has a light box for viewing transparencies built into the surface.

a fact of working life

When Nigel, an architect and surveyor, saw the empty, unfinished shell of this fifth-floor loft space, it was the huge main room flooded with light and the panoramic views that convinced him to move out of his traditional terrace house and live here with his teenage son. As the room became the hub of his home and working life, he placed his desk in a prime position, just off-centre in the space, close to one of the windows. He reasoned that if work was to be enjoyable and very much a part of his life, it should be incorporated into the living space.

The interior palette is simple and restrained, comprising natural concrete and bare brick, some areas of white-painted plasterwork and a light oak floor. The furniture and furnishings echo these neutral colours, and cupboards are finished in a pewter colour to match the metal window frames. Curtains and blinds are omitted from the windows, so that Nigel and his son can enjoy views of the city day and night on three sides of the apartment.

The design of the office hinges on the quartet of handsome, contemporary-style desks that fit neatly together to make an enormous workstation. Below the desks there are capacious filing cabinets, with space enough to be devoted to the different areas of Nigel's life: there is one for surveying, one for architecture, and others for home-related paperwork and his passion for fishing.

RIGHT *Proving that Nigel has made his working life an integral part of his domestic life, the large four-desk workstation sits just off-centre in the room, next to the dining table, which doubles as a conference table. Soft seating areas are positioned to the right, and there is a long outdoor terrace to the left of the workspace.*

OPPOSITE *The large workstation takes pride of place next to the horizontal windows of this former industrial building. Seen in the foreground is the dining/conference area. Between the two, a floor panel contains electrical sockets and phone and ISDN points to supply the desk.*

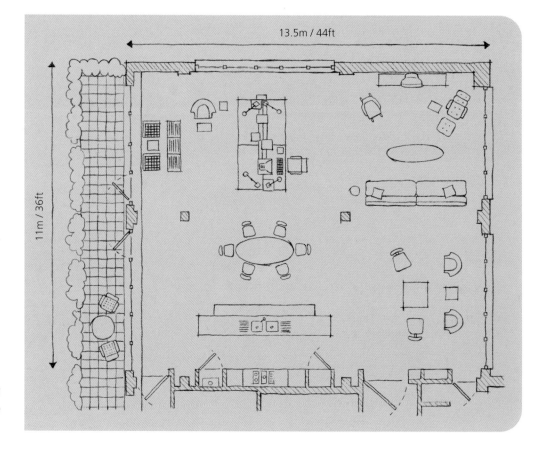

13.5m / 44ft

11m / 36ft

TOP LEFT *The walls are lined from floor to ceiling with cupboards providing lots of storage for files and magazines.*

ABOVE *This range of double-height cupboards is a neat storage solution; it also makes a stylish room divider, separating the working and living area from the kitchen.*

LEFT *The desktop is generously lit with natural light flowing in unobstructed through the large industrial windows. This can be boosted with a series of beautiful modern task lights, which are swung into position and angled to wherever they are most needed.*

OPPOSITE *The industrial aesthetic makes a crisp and hard-edged space. This side of the main living room could quite easily be mistaken for a design studio; in the other half of the room the space is softened with upholstered chairs and a sofa.*

Suspended above the back of the worktop are platforms for the computer monitor, task lights and any small items in regular use. Swing-out arms carry the telephones. All the electrical wiring, including the ISDN and telephone lines, is fed into channels built into the desk, which lead to floor sockets. Nigel's interest in collecting classic modern furniture led him to buy an elegant chrome and leather desk chair designed by Charles and Ray Eames, the design duo who also produced the distinctive plywood chairs that Nigel uses as both dining and conference table furniture.

Anticipating extensive storage needs, Nigel designed in cupboard and shelving space all over the apartment. He wanted to avoid the common problems experienced in traditional homes where rooms are cluttered with coat racks, cupboards and wardrobes, and, instead, he has used cupboards to mark off different areas or positioned them in subtle ways so that they disappear into the walls. Materials are simple MDF panels, which have been spray painted. A wall of shoulder-height cupboards acts as a room divider between the dining and kitchen areas, while elsewhere floor-to-ceiling cupboards line the walls and are used for storing files and folders. A lowered ceiling built over the bedrooms, bathroom and shower room is precisely two archive box files in height. It is reached by a ladder and well lit so that Nigel can read the clearly marked files, stored neatly in alphabetical order. While Nigel is careful about ordering his storage, he has a healthy attitude to everyday office untidiness and accepts that there will be times when the workstation will be chaotic – that is just a fact of working life.

garden cabin

OPPOSITE *The floor, walls and ceiling are lined with wood, giving a rustic appearance, which is in stark contrast to the contemporary desktop and office chair. The structure can be seen as either a sophisticated garden shed or a modern-day interpretation of a log cabin.*

BELOW *The plan shows how the worksurface is cantilevered through the wall and stretches out into the garden. At the back of the room, the daybed juts out similarly. On warm days, it is a real pleasure to sit outside on the decking, which is an integral part of the design.*

While most people are content with a shed at the bottom of their garden, Rosemary, a writer, wanted something more. She envisaged a space that was worth lingering in; a place to read and think and write. After discussing her plans with friends, they recommended an architect they thought would be ideal for her project. When client and architect met, it was clear the friends were right.

The design process took an unusual route. No drawings were produced for weeks. Instead, the two of them sat, surrounded by piles of architecture books and magazines, and talked through dozens of ideas. They discussed the appeal of log cabins, primitive huts, garden sheds as well as caravans, and collected together a series of ideas and details to include in the final building. They both agreed that miniaturization was the key: making the most of small spaces; fold-out furniture; tiny cupboards that open to reveal useful pockets of space.

Gradually a design evolved and emerged, as a cross between a garden shed and a grown-up play house. The result is every writer's dream – a garden pavilion that is peaceful and inspiring.

The construction materials couldn't have been more straightforward. The cabin is built from sheets of douglas fir plywood, hung on to a timber frame, which have been finished with a stainer-preservative that soaks into the surface. In time, the panels will weather, taking on a muted, silvery finish to blend in with the garden decking. Sheets of plywood have been used on the inside, too. The walls are insulated and electric radiators have been installed, so that the cabin can be used during the winter.

To create views and to prevent the cabin from feeling claustrophobic, the architect has designed in a collection of large and small windows. The main window surrounds the desktop, which has been dramatically pushed out through the wall so that it juts into the garden. It sits in a glass bay, cleverly built as a frameless structure with a small sloping roof, with views through the garden towards the back of the house. A clerestory – a horizontal band of glass at the top of the walls – brings in lots of indirect sunlight and makes the roof appear to float over the structure. At the back of the cabin there are small square windows, which give snapshot-like views into the trees behind.

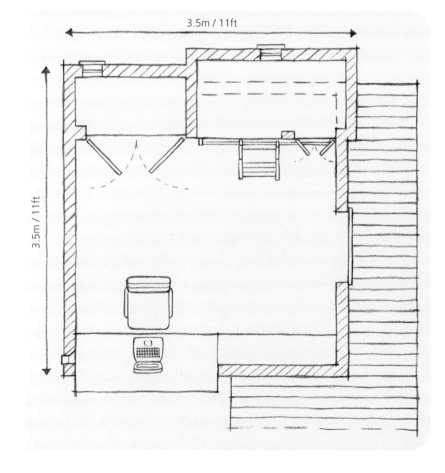

3.5m / 11ft

3.5m / 11ft

RIGHT *A kitchen-in-a-box. The architect's inspiration comes from the compact designs for caravan, boat and train interiors, where lots of pockets of space are built in. Even the kettle has to share space with office equipment such as a printer.*

BELOW *Underneath the daybed, cupboard doors open to reveal ample storage space for files and Rosemary's treasured collection of vinyl records.*

The desk is undeniably the focus of the cabin, with the generous worksurface stretching into the garden. It usefully contains three deep rectangular slots for stowing small office items. Above the desk, a single bookshelf runs the entire length of the top of the wall. Rosemary sits at a comfortable high-quality, leather-upholstered office chair, and there is also a low bench next to the desk.

Along the back wall there is a range of built-in cupboards and a daybed. The cupboards open to reveal a small kitchen area and shelving. Borrowing from the Romany caravan and old-fashioned train

sleeping compartments, the daybed is enclosed on three sides and reached by a small ladder. To echo the way in which the desktop bursts through the front wall, the daybed is similarly cantilevered out through the back wall. The daybed is an integral part of the design yet it is in complete contrast to the rest of the cabin. Lined with decadent scarlet upholstery, it is Rosemary's one area of indulgence. When there is time, this is the most glorious place to relax and listen to music.

Since Rosemary wanted to keep clutter in the cabin to a minimum, she has retained the elemental feel of the structure. She has imposed a strict work discipline and likes to start and end the day with a clear desk. The discipline has been set not because she is naturally tidy; her inclination is to be messy, but here she was presented with the opportunity to gain real control over the contents of the office. Each morning she brings from the house only those materials she needs – including portable computer and printer – for the project in hand. There is no telephone, no way of hearing the house doorbell and there are no visitors. The perfect writer's retreat.

OPPOSITE *The writer's cabin in its garden setting, showing the desktop extending through the exterior wall and, on top, the beginnings of a shaggy turf roof, which not only looks eco-friendly but insulates, too.*

RIGHT *Reminiscent of a Romany caravan, the inviting, enclosed daybed provides an ideal place for rest and contemplation; there is even a tiny window to look through at the trees beyond. There is a huge element of fantasy in the cabin's design, even though it is built in a city garden; it is hard to imagine the busy world in action just yards away.*

rooftop retreat

When interior designer Hanne Lise first went to view her city-centre apartment and saw the roof terrace, she knew that it was exactly what she needed. In her previous home, she had made do with an office squeezed into the kitchen, but here she spotted the potential to build a rooftop work pavilion with great views of the city skyline.

The pavilion is a simple wooden structure with lots of glazing, built in the style of a summer house. This compact space, which measures no more than 13 square metres (140 square feet), has become by far the most popular room of the apartment. Hanne Lise says that working in it makes her feel on top of the world. But it is not just a dual-use space; it has become a multi-purpose room, providing an office, sleep-over accommodation for guests and a sunny summer dining area.

To enhance the openness and natural light, the interior is painted off-white. There are seven doors in total, which transform the space from a closed room to an open gazebo. The minimal office is built along one wall of the structure. It comprises a tall, floor-to-ceiling cupboard and a desk that is large enough for spreading out interior design plans and drawings – Hanne Lise likes to work the traditional way by drawing directly on to paper.

When designing the storage cupboard, Hanne Lise measured every item it would contain, from boxes and files to the fax machine, and designed shelving to fit exactly. Some of the shelves, such as the one carrying the printer, can be pulled out when the equipment is in use, and then slid back once work has finished. Because she wanted to keep the office as low-impact and clutter-free as possible,

RIGHT *A tiny space cleverly organized to cope with work and play. The office area is contained on one side, leaving room for a sofa that doubles as a guest bed.*

OPPOSITE TOP LEFT *The rooftop pavilion has seven doors, making it a wonderfully light and airy place to work or entertain.*

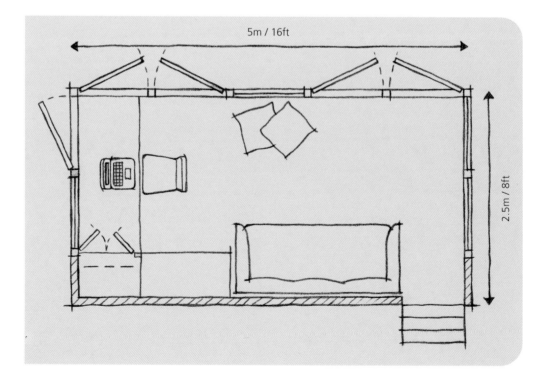

5m / 16ft

2.5m / 8ft

LEFT *Well-ordered cupboard space has been custom-made to fit files, folders and storage boxes exactly. Some of the shelves, such as that acommodating the printer, pull out when the equipment is in use, then slide back when work is over.*

BELOW *Hanne Lise says she feels on top of the world when she is sitting at her desk looking out over the city rooftops. Fabric blinds in the ceiling give a tented feel to the space, but they are practical as well, keeping out the more extreme effects of the sun in summer.*

Hanne Lise keeps her fabric and paint swatches in a downstairs cupboard, which she also uses as storage for archive files on past projects.

The desk is cleverly designed in two parts. The section closest to the cupboard is fixed permanently in place, but the other part can be picked up and moved and used as a dining table. For large dinner parties, Hanne Lise adds a lightweight folding table.

The cream-coloured linen blinds are an essential part of the design. They stretch across the glass roof to give the room a tented feel and are also fitted to each of the doors. The fabric diffuses the light and provides welcome shade from the summer sun.

rooftop retreat

school work

One of the most desirable features of this large, open-plan home, which was originally part of a Victorian school, is the natural light that floods in through the high windows. The school, which dates from the 1870s, was in the process of being divided into half a dozen separate living units when the current owners first viewed it. Even then, in its unconverted state, disguised by layers of dirt and grime, the space had instant and lasting appeal. For the duration of the refurbishment and renovation, the natural light was considered a major priority and treated as a precious commodity.

The home is owned by Nik, who is an architect, and Suzsi, a textile designer. Nik's own architecture practice was commissioned to turn one of the units into a home for the couple and their son, Louis. The brief also included making a workplace for Suzsi.

Nik and Suzsi found the school development just before Louis was born. Suzsi had been working in a very small studio and, with the arrival of her child, wanted to work at home. By cutting out two hours' commuting every day, she would have more time to look after Louis and the opportunity to work far more flexible hours.

Building work included the removal of the old ceilings above the original classrooms, to reveal the true grandeur and drama of the space. The unit was opened to the apex of the roof, highlighting the ornate rose-design window set into the gable end. The plans for the interior kept the double-height space open over the kitchen and dining room, but introduced a mezzanine floor above the sitting area and under the rooflights. This was to become Suzsi's new studio, an ideal place for her to work on finely

RIGHT *Workbenches and a desktop are arranged around the perimeter of the studio space, to keep the centre of the room clear and allow natural light to cascade through the glass floor into the sitting area below.*

OPPOSITE *The huge, airy space of the main living area, with the studio mezzanine seemingly floating in mid-air. The original Victorian rose window is carved from stone.*

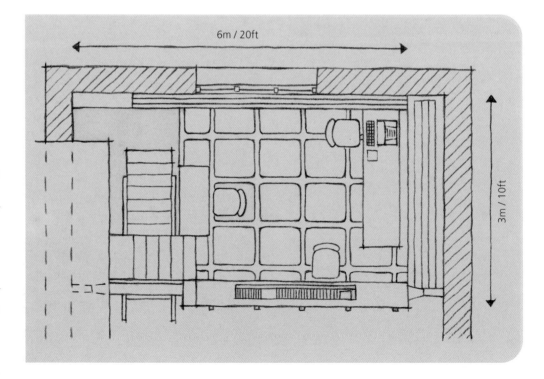

6m / 20ft

3m / 10ft

detailed textile projects. The abundant natural light not only makes it easier to see the close-knit work, but it also gives true colour rendition, which is vital.

Steel beams have been inserted close to the base of the timber trusses to span the space and create Suzsi's studio. The beams support an open steelwork grid, into which is set the unusual glass floor. The glass panels slot into the steel frame and are fixed in place with silicon to make a smooth, seamless surface. Nik's architecture practice has established a reputation for its adventurous use of glass and this project provided an ideal opportunity to explore its potential and try something very new. The see-through floor is designed to allow natural light to reach the sitting area below. It also gives Suzsi the chance to keep an eye on Louis, now aged five, as he plays in the open-plan living area while she works in the studio. As you look down, the view is dominated by the original pale beech floor, which was stripped back using an industrial sander.

The mezzanine studio is reached by an open-tread timber stair and, as you climb to the top, there are glimpses outside of the roof terrace and city skyline. The studio appears to float in space and its airiness is further underlined by its link to the roof terrace, accessed by a short, but extremely elegant, all-glass flight of stairs.

To furnish Suzsi's studio, Nik placed benches around three sides of the space and kept the centre empty. The worktops are fixed on to a framework

A room with a view – downwards to the family sitting room. Suzsi's ergonomic chair rests on the transparent glass floor that is slotted into the steel grid.

LEFT *Workbenches surround three sides of the mezzanine, looking down into the open-plan living space. Knitting machines are firmly bolted to the bench – anything falling from that height could cause serious damage.*

BELOW *A bird's-eye view from the roof terrace into the studio. Suzsi's desk is on the left and the glass stair that links studio and roof terrace is on the right.*

of upright steel posts, which are securely bolted to the floor. These posts also act as conduits for telephone and electrical cabling, and there are sockets fixed at worktop height. At the back of the benches, wire mesh is fixed to the posts to create safety balustrading. The mesh is an open weave to let the all-important light pass through, but the holes are sufficiently small to prevent anything dropped from falling to the floor below.

Suzsi's work as a textile designer involves designing and making samples of woven cloth and embroidery patterns for large fashion houses. The tools of her trade include computerized electronic knitting machines, plus a personal computer for design work and office administration. The materials that she uses on a regular basis include a rainbow of coloured yarns, which are wound on to cone-shaped spools. These yarns are stored on a raised shelf and bring extra colour and interest to the

studio. To keep her work space uncluttered, Suzsi stores her complete range of yarns on the floor below, in the entrance hall. Instead of packing them away, she displays them in rows on open shelves, which creates an interesting colour and textural contrast with the exposed brick wall behind.

Storage in the studio has deliberately been kept to a minimum to avoid obscuring the beauty of the building and to maximize the natural light. One of the early plans included building shelving on the underside of the sloping ceiling plane, but the idea was dropped as the space evolved. Instead, remote storage for files and folders that are no longer in regular use has been found in a combined playroom and guestroom, where a cupboard houses a couple of integrated filing cabinets.

Crossing the entire span of the mezzanine is the workbench with knitting machines bolted into position, for obvious safety reasons. Suzsi's desktop workbench holds her personal computer. The space below the bench is stacked with opaque plastic boxes on wheels, filled with dozens of colourful knitted and embroidered samples. The studio chairs were chosen by the architecture practice using the best possible research method: over a period of several weeks, everyone working in the practice tried out a series of chairs, and this particular model emerged as the most supportive and comfortable.

Suzsi has an additional small worktop at the foot of the glass stairs, which is also a peaceful spot for contemplation and enjoying the city skyline. On warm days the enormous rooflight panels can be slid open, so that the glass staircase leads straight out to the roof terrace.

ABOVE *To maximize space in the mezzanine studio, most of Suzsi's yarns are kept on open shelves in the hallway below, creating an attractive display of colour.*

OPPOSITE *This blissful working environment is a far cry from Suzsi's previous cramped studio. The enormous sliding doors open on to the roof terrace, which is reached by the amazing, transparent glass stairway.*

working life

To be a successful homeworker, there
has to be some framework for the day
and for the weeks, even months, ahead

getting motivated

Working at home day after day requires a fairly high degree of self-discipline. Without a boss to watch the clock and set the agenda, it can be tough to get up and get going every morning. There are many temptations to overcome; it is extremely easy to be distracted from accomplishing the tasks you have set yourself by pursuing more pleasurable activities, such as taking the dog for a walk or raiding the fridge. Of course, being a homeworker means that your time is your own, but that only works within the realms of practicality. There is obviously no point starting work at 6pm if you need to speak to clients who, by that time, have come to the end of their working day and gone home.

The best way of organizing your time is to find a balance between work and play, so that you can complete all your work on time and build in trips away from home, at the same time keeping a close eye on your income to make sure that it meets expectations. Finding the balance can be tricky, and if you are just starting out as a homeworker, you will need several months at least before you manage to establish the right rhythm and are able to reap all the benefits of working from home.

make the most of being a homeworker

REWARD YOURSELF with time off in lieu if you have had to work late or long hours on a big project.

SET NEW CHALLENGES and learn new skills, so that you don't get bored.

TRAVEL OUTSIDE the rush hour when the fares are usually lower and it is less crowded.

JOIN A GYM and consider off-peak membership, which is cheaper and you will have the place to yourself.

GO TO THE SUPERMARKET in the morning when there are fewer shoppers.

BOOK THE OCCASIONAL midweek break, and remember how lucky you are to work at home.

managing time

Time management is all about being kind to yourself. Get it right and you will be able to set realistic goals, allocate enough time to achieve them and ensure you have a life outside work. The result that we are all after is job satisfaction, reduced stress and an enhanced quality of life. By making the choice to work at home you have taken control of your time. You can now decide what you do, as well as when and how to do it.

Before you rush out to buy wall charts and calendars, take a broad view of your lifestyle and job. Ask yourself some basic questions. How much do I need to earn? How do I want to work? How much time do I want to spend working? What are the other demands on my time? Are there things I would like to make more time for, such as learning a new language or going away at weekends?

Then focus on how you work. Take time to analyse and understand when and how you work best. By tuning in to your natural body rhythms, you can plan the day to take advantage of your most productive time and build in breaks when you are at a low ebb. Everyone has their own working rhythm and their own way of getting started. I know of freelance homeworkers who get up at 6.30am, go straight to the local gym for an hour, take a light breakfast and then work without a break until mid-afternoon. They then stop dead and that is it for the day. Others enjoy the freedom of getting up late, taking a leisurely breakfast, reading the paper and eventually sitting at their desks as late as 11am, but they are fully prepared to work until 7 or 8 in the evening. Others divide their day into segments to fit around the needs of children or other commitments.

Whichever work style you adopt, provided that it suits your temperament, your life and your bank balance, it will be an unmitigated success.

In designing a work schedule, first decide what you need to accomplish. Once you have a clear idea of the income you need, determine how you find the work to bring in the money. You will need to set aside time for meetings, sending out letters, attending trade shows, organizing advertising. Then take a look at what your job involves. Identify the tasks you will need to perform in an average week, and make sure you allocate enough time for everything. Do you expect to take on a mixture of long and short projects? Will there be large gaps between projects? Are there measures you can take to even out the work flow? After being self-employed for a while, it becomes easier to estimate how long tasks will take, but in the early days it is best to overestimate, to allow time for error.

Whatever your profession, you will need to build in a realistic amount of time for all the extra tasks associated with working on your own, such as visiting the post office, buying stationery, completing accounts, reading newspapers, attending training courses, and so on.

Finally, make room for everyday life. Set aside time for such activities as visiting the supermarket and taking children to school, but, most important of all, identify the cut-off point when work has to end and stick to it. One of the commonest problems experienced by homeworkers is that the lines between work and free time tend to merge. Many find themselves at their desks late into the night and allow work to spill over into weekends and holidays.

This is not fair on you or anyone else. A sensible time-management plan should build in time enough for work and for play. Make sure that there are chunks of the day or week when family and friends know that you are at work and not to be disturbed. Equally, make sure work colleagues know not to contact you at those times earmarked for family and friends, or just for yourself.

A time-management plan should be as user-friendly as possible. Fixed timetables leave no room for flexibility and the unexpected, but without a structure you will find that the days pass in a haze and you have little sense of what has been finished and what remains to be done. Both extremes diminish any feeling of job satisfaction and are also likely to lead to stress and anxiety.

time management checklist

ASSESS how much work you need to generate to meet your desired income.

IDENTIFY what you need to do to ensure a regular flow of work: should you arrange weekly/monthly meetings to drum up new business, send out regular letters, advertise in trade magazines, reserve exhibition stands?

KEEP A CHART to plan and block in work for the year; include holidays and mark in relevant trade events, such as major exhibitions or fairs.

MAKE A SKETCH plan for the next couple of months to visualize what is in store so that you can build in time for preparation and not leave everything to the last minute. Planning combats the excesses of stress.

AT THE START of each week, take 15 to 20 minutes to list the tasks that need to be completed in that week, with estimates of how long they will take. Include small jobs, such as writing letters and buying extra stationery, and be realistic about what you will be able to achieve.

PRIORITIZE TASKS and block in work on your diary pages; if you have promised a delivery on Friday, make sure you have time to honour that commitment. Reliability will help guarantee client loyalty and repeat business.

WHEN TAKING ON NEW WORK, assess how long it will take to accomplish and when it has to be delivered; refer to your chart or diary and make sure it fits in with your timetable. When assessing the time required to complete a big project, break it down into segments and estimate time for each part.

AVOID COMMITTING YOURSELF to a new project unless you are confident that it can be accomplished well and on time. As a general rule, clients prefer a commission to be refused than to have the work completed badly and late.

DO NOT rush small chores; it takes more than five minutes to write a letter and it is often worth spending half an hour to ensure you say exactly what you intend. Leave time for finishing touches, such as checking your spelling.

DO NOT put off doing difficult or unappealing tasks; delay can be stressful.

IF WORK DOES build up unexpectedly, have strategies in place for coping; hire in help or work all weekend to get the job done, and make sure it does not happen again.

MONITOR AND REVIEW your time planning to make sure your estimates are accurate.

home-office exercises

An active body is a healthy body, and anyone spending their working life at a desk should build in time to look after themselves and keep fit.

Research has shown that people who work at home tend to sit at their desks for longer periods than their office-based counterparts. Even with the best possible chair and ergonomically designed workstation, this can store up trouble in the joints and muscles, producing a stiff neck and shoulder muscles, a sore back, strained hands and arms, and even headaches, caused by eye-strain. Sitting still for hours is a bad idea, so it is important to build in breaks and opportunities for moving around, such as taking a walk at lunchtime.

To help keep you supple and prevent stiffness, the following simple exercises can be carried out at, or close to, your desk. Before you start work, do a warm-up exercise, and follow it with about 15 minutes of stretching and flexing the various parts of the body. Even though you may not be seated at your desk every minute of the day, by the end of it your body is likely to be slightly tense. So, once you stop working, spend around five minutes on the general stretching exercises, and finish with the warm-up routine. (If you have recently suffered a major illness or have any concerns about embarking on a new exercise regime, consult your general practitioner.)

warm up

Standing, shake your left hand for a few seconds (as if you were shaking off water), then shake the right hand. Shake both hands and arms together. Shake your left foot and ankle, then shake the right. Shake your shoulders and top half of your torso for a few seconds. Then, with legs slightly apart and arms at your side, roll your head as close as possible to your shoulders in a circular motion three times, then in the reverse direction three times. Remain standing and screw up your face muscles and hold for a few seconds, then work down through your whole body, tightening your neck, shoulders, arms, wrists, hands, upper torso, abdomen, buttocks, legs, ankles and toes in turn. Hold each position for a few seconds and release. Relax and repeat the exercise.

back

Standing with your legs slightly apart, stretch your arms above your head and point to the ceiling. Hold for a slow count of six. Relax. Repeat four times. For your upper back, stand up straight, clasp hands behind your head and slowly arch your back, bending the head backwards to look at the ceiling. Hold for up to five seconds. Relax and repeat twice.

shoulders, arms, neck

Standing, extend your left arm to the side, so that it is level with your shoulder. Slowly rotate your arm clockwise six times and then anticlockwise six times. Repeat the exercise with the right arm.

neck

Standing or seated, turn the head slowly to look over your left shoulder for five seconds, and then look to the right for five seconds. Repeat four times.

wrists and fingers

Standing or seated, stretch out the arms in front of the body and gently rotate the hands at the wrist so that the first finger of each hand draws circles in the air. Rotate both wrists six times in one direction and then in the other. Relax and repeat twice. With hands hanging down at your sides, clench both fists and hold for a slow count of three, then spread your fingers wide open for a slow count of three. Relax and repeat three times.

eyes

Give your eyes a break by occasionally looking away from your computer monitor and focusing on a distant object, at least 45m (50yds) away, for a few seconds. Then close your eyes for a few more seconds. Repeat the exercise three times.

general stretching

Stand with your legs slightly apart and raise both arms at the side of your body until they reach above your head. As you point to the ceiling, rise up on to the balls of your feet. Slowly lower your arms and return to standing with feet flat. Repeat this three times. Standing upright, with feet slightly apart and arms at your side, bend to the left and run your left hand down your left leg as far as you can. Repeat three times. Do the same bending to the right. Stand up straight, then slowly bend forward, letting your hands hang down in front of your body. If it feels comfortable, see if you can touch your toes. Stand up slowly. Repeat three times.

addresses

ARCHITECTS & DESIGNERS

a² 2000 Ltd
(see pages 108–9)
4th Floor, 191 Wardour Street
London W1V 3FA
Tel: 020 7494 3323

Brookes Stacey Randall
(see pages 142–7)
New Hibernia House
Winchester Walk
London SE1 9AG
Tel: 020 7403 0707

Formwork Architects
(see pages 116–19)
23 Warrington Crescent
London W9 1ED
Tel: 020 7266 5723

Hanne Lise Poli, pHa-Design
(see pages 140–1)
Via di Monterosi SNC
00069 Trevignano Romano
Italy
Tel: 00 39 333 458 5854

Littman Goddard Hogarth Ltd
(see pages 120–3)
12 Chelsea Wharf
London SW10
Tel: 020 7351 7871

Nigel Smith Architect
(see pages 132–5)
York Central
70 York Way
London N1 9AG
Tel: 020 7278 8802

Sarah Wigglesworth
(see pages 136–9)
10 Stock Orchard Street
London N7
Tel: 020 7607 9200

Royal Institute of British Architects
66 Portland Place
London W1N 4AD
Tel: 020 7580 5533

GENERAL BUILDING INFORMATION

Building Centre
26 Store Street
London WC1E 7BT
Tel: 020 7637 1022
(resource & display centre)

Business Design Centre
52 Upper Street
London N1 0QH
Tel: 020 7359 3535
(building trade & product showrooms)

Federation of Master Builders
Gordon Fisher House
14–15 Great James Street
London WC1N 3DP
Tel: 020 7242 7583

Interior Decorators & Designers
Association
1–4 Chelsea Harbour Design Centre
Lots Road
London SW10 0XE
Tel: 020 7349 0800
(professional association of interior
designers & decorators)

OFFICE FURNITURE
MANUFACTURERS & RETAILERS

Aram Designs
3 Kean Street
London WC2 4AT
Tel: 020 7240 3933
(contemporary furniture specialist)

Archiutti
69–73 Theobalds Road
London WC1X 8TA
Tel: 020 7831 6678
www.archiutti.co.uk
(office furniture specialist)

Boss Design
117 Wolverhampton Street
Dudley
West Midlands DY1 3AL
Tel: 01384 455570
www.boss-design.co.uk
(office furniture manufacturer)

Co-Existence
288 Upper Street
London N1
Tel: 020 7354 8817
www.coexistence.co.uk
(contemporary furniture specialist)

The Conran Shop
Michelin House
81 Fulham Road
London SW3 6RD
Tel: 020 7589 7401
www.conran.co.uk
(general contemporary furniture)

Dauphin
Peter Street
Blackburn
Lancashire BB1 5LH
Tel: 01254 52220
www.dauphin.plc.uk
(office furniture specialist)

Ergonomic Workstations
The Loft
55 Charlotte Road
London EC2A 3QF
Tel: 0800 521003
www.ergo-ws.com
(office furniture specialist)

Habitat
196 Tottenham Court Road
London W1P 9LD
Tel: 020 7631 3880
www.habitat.net
(has a home office collection)

Herman Miller
149 Tottenham Court Road
London W1P 0JA
Tel: 020 7388 7331
www.hermanmiller.com
(office furniture manufacturer)

Howe
24 Jaggard Way
London SW12 8SG
Tel: 020 8673 9777
(office furniture specialist)

Ikea
2 Drury Way
London NW10 0TH
Tel: 020 8208 5600
www.ikea.com
(has a home office collection)

John Lewis of Hungerford
Grove Technology Park
Downs View Road
Wantage
Oxon OX12 9FA
Tel: 01235 774300
www.v-home-office.co.uk
(all-in-one office units)

Knoll International
1 Lindsey Street
London EC1A 9PQ
Tel: 020 7236 6655
www.knollint.com
(office furniture specialist)

Living
16/17 Lionel Street
Birmingham B3 1AQ
Tel: 0121 236 8764
www.formspace.co.uk
(retailer of well-known makes of
home & office furniture)

Mufti
789 Fulham Road
London SW6 5HA
Tel: 020 7610 9123
www.mufti.co.uk
(contemporary furniture specialist)

Purves & Purves
80–1 Tottenham Court Road
London W1P 9HD
Tel: 020 7580 8223
www.purves.co.uk
(general contemporary furniture)

SCP
135–9 Curtain Road
London EC2A 3BX
Tel: 020 7739 1869
www.scp.co.uk
(contemporary furniture specialist)

Scott Howard Systems Furniture
Unit 2
New Rock Industrial Estate
Chilcompton
Somerset BA3 4JE
Tel: 01761 232997
www.scotthoward.co.uk
(office furniture specialist)

Space2
Silver City House
62 Brompton Road
London SW3 1BW
Tel: 0800 028 20 22
www.space2.com
(home office furniture specialist)

Steelcase Strafor
Newlands Drive
Poyle
Berkshire
Tel: 01753 680200
www.steelcase-europe.com
(office furniture specialist)

Vitra
30 Clerkenwell Road
London EC1
Tel: 020 7608 6200
www.vitra.com
(office furniture specialist)

STORAGE

Bisley Office Furniture
Northumberland House
155–7 Great Portland Street
London W1N 5FB
Tel: 020 7436 7111
www.bisley.com
(retailer of office storage)

Intoform Ltd
12 Liberty Way
Attleborough Fields Industrial Estate
Nuneaton
Warwickshire CV11 6RZ
Tel: 024 76 347 777
(retailer of office storage)

The Maine Group
Home Park
Kings Langley
Hertfordshire WD4 8LZ
Tel: 01923 260411
www.maine.co.uk
(manufacturer of office storage)

LIGHTING

Altima
2–10 Telford Way
Westway Estate
London W3 7XX
Tel: 020 8600 3500
www.altima.co.uk

Anglepoise
Unit 5, Enfield Industrial Area
Redditch
Worcestershire B97 6DR
Tel: 01527 63771
www.anglepoise.co.uk

Artemide
106 Great Russell Street
London WC1
Tel: 020 7631 5200
www.artemide.com

Erco
38 Dover Street
London W1
Tel: 020 7408 0320
www.erco.com

Flos Ltd
31 Lisson Grove
London NW1 6UB
Tel: 020 7258 0600
www.flos.net

Hacel Lighting
The Silverlink
Wallsend
Tyne & Wear NE28 9ND
Tel: 0191 280 9911
www.hacel.co.uk

Iguzzini
Unit 310, Business Design Centre
Upper Street
London N1
Tel: 020 8646 4141
www.iguzzini.co.uk

La Conch Lighting
4 The Chase Centre
Chase Road
London NW10 6QD
Tel: 020 8961 0313
www.laconch.co.uk

Lucent
7a Coppetts Road
London N10
Tel: 020 8442 0880
www.lucent-lighting.co.uk

FLOORING

The Amtico Company
Kingfield Road
Coventry CV6 5PL
Tel: 020 7629 6258
(London showroom)
www.amtico.com
(vinyl flooring)

Crucial Trading Ltd
PO Box 11, Duke Place
Kidderminster
Worcestershire DY10 2JR
Tel: 01562 825656
(natural fibre floorcoverings)

Fired Earth
Twyford Mills, Oxford Road
Alderbury
Oxfordshire OX17 3HP
Tel: 01295 812088
www.firedearth.co.uk
(glazed floor & wall tiles, paints)

Forbo-Nairn Ltd
PO Box 1
Kirkcaldy
Fife KY1 2SB
Tel: 01592 643777
www.forbo-nairn.co.uk
(linoleum in sheet & tile form)

Junckers Ltd
Wheaton Court Commercial Centre
Wheaton Road
Witham
Essex CM8 3UJ
Tel: 01376 517512
www.junckers.dk
(hardwood flooring)

Kahrs (UK) Ltd
Timberlane Estate
Quarry Lane
Chichester
West Sussex PO19 2FJ
Tel: 01243 778747
www.kahrs.se
(hardwood flooring)

Naturestone
Silwood Road
Sunninghill
Berkshire SL5 0PZ
Tel: 01344 627 617
www.stone.co.uk
(stone flooring)

Stone Age
14 King's Road
Clifton
Bristol BS8 4AB
Tel: 0117 923 8180
www.estone.co.uk
(stone flooring)

Walcot Reclamation
108 Walcot Street
Bath
Avon
Tel: 01225 44404
www.walcot.com
(reclaimed timber, stone & ceramic
flooring)

PAINTS

Crown Paints
PO Box 37
Crown House
Hollins Road
Darwen
Lancashire BB3 OBG
Tel: 01254 704 951
www.akzonobel.com

Dulux
Tel: 01753 550555
www.dulux.co.uk

Lakeland Paints
Unit 19
Lake District Business Park
Kendal
Cumbria LA9 6NH
Tel: 01539 732866
www.ecospaint.com
(natural, solvent-free paints
& varnishes)

MISCELLANEOUS

Association for Environment
Conscious Building
PO Box 32
Llandysul
Carmarthen SA44 5ZA
Tel: 01559 370908
www.aecb.net

Construction Resources
16 Great Guildford Street
London SE1 0HS
Tel: 020 7450 2211
www.ecoconstruct.com
(ecological builder's merchant)

Draks Shutters
Draks Industries
Unit 316
Heyford Park
Upper Heyford
Oxfordshire OX6 3HA
www.sin.be/bosmans_draks
(shutters & blinds)

Ecomerchant
The Old Filling Station
Head Hill Road
Goodnestone
Nr Faversham
Kent ME13 9BY
Tel: 01795 530130
www.ecomerchant.co.uk
(ecological builder's merchant)

Home Business Alliance
www.hba.org.uk
(website with information on all
aspects of working at home)

Knobs & Knockers
10 Churchill Business Park
Seeds Lane
Aintree
Liverpool 9L9 9HD
Tel: 0151 523 4900
ww.knobsandknockers.co.uk

index

acknowledgments

The author and publisher would particularly like to thank all those who allowed their home offices to be photographed and discussed in this book. The following organizations kindly supplied materials for the special photography:

Ordning & Reda, 21–2 New Row, London WC2 4LA (Tel: 020 7240 8090); Nicole Farhi Home, 17 Clifford Street, London W1X 1RG (Tel: 020 7494 9051); Conran Collection, 12 Conduit Street, London W1R 9TD (Tel: 020 7399 0710); Bureau, 10 Great Newport Street, London WC2H 7JA (Tel: 020 7379 8898); SCP, 135–9 Curtain Road, London EC2A 3BX (Tel: 020 7739 1869); The Frozen Fountain, Amsterdam (0031 2062 29373); Menno Kroon, Amsterdam (0031 2067 91950); Mac House 1st Applestore, Amsterdam (0031 3484 84999). Thanks also to Herman Miller, who provided information on ergonomic design; Janine Furness; Gillian Preston; Gilbert; Sharon Amos; Lindsay Porter; Kathie Gill.

The publisher would like to thank the following photographers and agencies for their kind permission to reproduce the photographs in this book:

4 Tim Evan-Cook/Elle Decoration; 8–10 Ray Main/Mainstream; 11 Wayne Vincent/The Interior Archive (Design: Leo Santos-Shaw); 12 Hulton Getty Picture Collection; 14 Nick Ivins/Nowicka Stern; 16 Lena Koller/IMS Bildbyra; 17 Hotze Eisma/Eigen Huis & Interieur/VNU; 19 Alberto Emanuele Piovano; 22 Winfried Heinze/Red Cover; 23 Peter Aprahamian/Living Etc; 24 Dennis Brandsma/VT Wonen/VNU; 25 Hotze Eisma/Taverne Agency; 27 Ray Main/Mainstream (Babylon Design); 28 Guy Obijn; 29 Peter Aprahamian/Dulux Colour magazine; 30 Grazia Branco/Iketrade; 31 Jan Verlinde (Architect: Carlo Seminck); 32 above Trevor Mein/Belle/Arcaid (Architect: Andrew Parr); 32 below Peter Clarke/Vogue Living; 33 Hotze Eisma/Eigen Huis & Interieur/VNU; 34–5 Alexander van Berge; 36 Gilles de Chabaneix/Marie Claire Maison (Stylist: C. Ardouin); 37 Richard Powers/Elle Decoration; 39 Philippe Costes/Marie Claire Maison (Stylists: Postic/Reyre); 40 Andrew Wood/The Interior Archive (Owner: Brun Ma Siy); 42 Dennis Brandsma/Eigen Huis & Interieur/VNU; 43 Marie Pierre Morel/Marie Claire Maison (Stylist: C Puech/M Kalt); 44 Tom Leighton/Living Etc/IPC Syndication; 46 Trevor Mein/Vogue Living; 47 Chris Gascoigne/View (Architect: Simon Conder Associates); 48 left Alexander van Berge/Elle Wonen; 48 right Peter Aprahamian (Architect: Nico Rensch); 49 Daniel Ward/Ikea Room/John Brown Contract Publishing Ltd; 50 Ray Main/Mainstream (Architect: Duncan Baker Brown); 51–2 Ray Main/Mainstream; 52–3 Verne Fotografie (GVC Company – BXL); 55 Tom Leighton/Living Etc/IPC Syndications; 56 Nick Pope/Living Etc/IPC Syndication; 57 Guy Obijn; 58 Helén Pe/IMS Bildbyra; 60–1 Peter Cook/View (Architect: Fiona McLean); 62 Tim Evan-Cook/Elle Decoration; 63 above Paul Warchol; 63 below Ray Main/Mainstream (Babylon Design); 65 Grazia Branco/Iketrade; 66 Trevor Richards/Living Etc/IPC Syndication; 67 Andrew Wood/The Interior Archive (Architect: Spencer Fung); 68 Hotze Eisma/Eigen Huis & Interieurs/VNU; 68–9 Matteo Piazzo; 69 Dennis Brandsma/Eigen Huis & Interieurs/VNU; 70 Trevor Mein/Vogue Living; 72 Dreyer/Hensley; 73 Paul Whicheloe (Reproduced by permission from House Beautiful, © January 2000. The Hearst Corporation); 74 Chris Everard/Elle Decoration; 76 Clive Frost (Architect: Fiona McLean); 77 left Winfried Heinze/Red Cover; 77 right Grazia Branco/Iketrade; 78 left Hotze Eisma/Eigen Huis & Interieur/VNU; 78 right Ray Main/Mainstream; 80 Solvi Dos Santos; 81 Catherine Bogart/Deborah Berke Architects; 82 Alexander van Berge/Elle Wonen; 83 Ray Main/Mainstream (Architect: Duncan Baker Brown); 84 Peter Cook/View; 85 Ray Main/Mainstream; 88 Eduardo Munoz/La Casa de Marie Claire/Picture Press; 89 Ray Main/Mainstream; 90 Eduardo Munoz/The Interior Archive (Owner: Santi Nieto); 93 left Paul Warchol; 93 right Ray Main/Mainstream; 94 Alexander van Berge/VT Wonen/VNU; 96 Henry Wilson/The Interior Archive (Owner: Milbus); 97 Tim Young/Living Etc/IPC Syndication; 98–9 Paul Warchol; 100 left Alexander van Berge/VT Wonen/VNU; 100 right Guy Bouchet/Marie Claire Maison (Stylist: M Kalt); 101 Dennis Brandsma/VT Wonen/VNU; 102 Edina van der Wyck/The Interior Archive (Designer: Atlanta Bartlett); 103 Jan Verlinde (Architect: Nathalie van Reeth); 104–5 Trevor Mein/Belle/Arcaid (Architect: John Wardle); 105 above Henry Wilson/The Interior Archive (Owner: Vincent Mazzucci); 105 below Dreyer/Hensley; 109 Clive Frost (a² 2000); 141 Hotze Eisma/Taverne Agency (Stylist: Hanne Lise Poli); 148 Tim Evan-Cook/Elle Decoration; 150 Philippe Costes/ Marie Claire Maison (Stylists: Postic/Reyre); 153 Patric Johansson/IMS Bildbyra.

Every effort has been made to trace the copyright holders and we apologize in advance for any unintentional omission and would be pleased to insert the appropriate acknowledgment in any subsequent edition.

The following photographs have been specially taken for Conran Octopus by:

Winfried Heinze (Stylist: Abigail Ahern): 2, 7, 20, 41, 86, 106, 116–19 (Architects: Jeremy Peacock/Formwork), 120–3 (Architects: Littman Goddard Hogarth Ltd; Double 'H' Loft Conversion Specialists 01483 562252), 124–7, 132–5 (Architect: Nigel Smith), 136–9 (Architect: Sarah Wigglesworth), 142–7 (Architects: Brookes Stacey Randall). Hotze Eisma (Stylist: Linda Loenen; Assistant stylist: Anouk Brands): 110–16, 128–31.